Swift Recipes for iOS Developers

Real-Life Code from App Store Apps

Alexander Nekrasov

Apress®

Swift Recipes for iOS Developers: Real-Life Code from App Store Apps

Alexander Nekrasov
Moscow, Russia

ISBN-13 (pbk): 978-1-4842-8097-3   ISBN-13 (electronic): 978-1-4842-8098-0
https://doi.org/10.1007/978-1-4842-8098-0

Managing Director, Apress Media LLC: Welmoed Spahr
Acquisitions Editor: Aaron Black
Development Editor: James Markham
Coordinating Editor: Jessica Vakili

Distributed to the book trade worldwide by Springer Science+Business Media New York, 1 NY Plaza, New York, NY 10004. Phone 1-800-SPRINGER, fax (201) 348-4505, e-mail orders-ny@springer-sbm.com, or visit www.springeronline.com. Apress Media, LLC is a California LLC and the sole member (owner) is Springer Science + Business Media Finance Inc (SSBM Finance Inc). SSBM Finance Inc is a **Delaware** corporation.

For information on translations, please e-mail booktranslations@springernature.com; for reprint, paperback, or audio rights, please e-mail bookpermissions@springernature.com.

Apress titles may be purchased in bulk for academic, corporate, or promotional use. eBook versions and licenses are also available for most titles. For more information, reference our Print and eBook Bulk Sales web page at http://www.apress.com/bulk-sales.

Any source code or other supplementary material referenced by the author in this book is available to readers on the Github repository: https://github.com/Apress/Swift-Recipes-for-iOS-Developers. For more detailed information, please visit http://www.apress.com/source-code.

Printed on acid-free paper

Table of Contents

About the Author

Alexander Nekrasov wrote his first line of code 27 years ago when he was eight years old and could see himself thriving as a software developer ever since. In 2008, he graduated from university with a diploma with honors as a System Engineer. By that point, he had already been working in the IT field for three years. In 2013, he wrote his first iOS app, and in 2014, he switched completely to mobile development. Almost ten years of freelance experience has given Alex an opportunity to work on many interesting projects and earn real-life experience. Alex runs a succesful blog where he writes about mobile development.

About the Technical Reviewer

Felipe Laso is a Senior Systems Engineer working at Lextech Global Services. He's also an aspiring game designer/programmer. You can follow him on Twitter at @iFeliLM or on his blog.

Acknowledgments

I want to thank everyone who has helped me with this book and made it possible for me to write it. All my university teachers, the authors of the books I've read and the teachers of the online courses I've watched, the bloggers, and thousands of people on Stack Overflow who have helped me gain the knowledge I have now.

I want to thank all my clients and bosses who have assigned me tasks that I couldn't do then, pushing me to learn further, and my fellow developers who wrote good code that I could read and learn from.

Special thanks go to my mother *Nina Nekrasova*, who, during the process of writing this book, has asked me how I was doing and if I was fitting my deadline every time we met, as if I was still a child and this was part of my homework.

And I got the biggest help and support from my wife *Gaby Prestes*, who patiently read every chapter of this book, corrected my grammar mistakes, and gave valuable feedback not even being a programmer herself. Thank you, Gaby. Without you, this book would have never happened.

How to Use This Book

The answer depends on your current level of knowledge on Swift.

If you're new to Swift and iOS/iPadOS platforms, you need to learn the Swift basics first. Make sure you can answer these questions before you dive into this book:

- What is a class and what's the difference between a class and a struct?

- How to run one or another branch of code depending on different conditions?

- How to run the same fragment of code multiple times?

- What is a nib/xib and a storyboard?

- How to declare a function or a variable?

- What's the difference between let and var?

You know the answers? Then you're good to go!

The simplest way to try Swift code is a Playground. You can create one in Xcode instead of a project. A Playground can contain one or more files; you can declare classes, variables, constants, and functions there. Basically, it's the same as a project, except that it won't compile into an executable. In a Swift Playground, you can run code without an iOS device or simulator, and you'll see the content of all variables without setting breakpoints.

If you're at the beginning of your Swift learning journey, it will be better for you to type the code instead of copying and pasting it. While typing, you're actively learning.

If you know other programming languages already, it will be much easier. But even if that's not the case, Swift is not a bad option to start with.

If you already know Swift but haven't written your own app yet, try to do so. Think of this: Which app would you like to have on your iPhone or iPad? It doesn't matter if such app already exists – make your own version of it! You can even publish it on the App Store in the end. Unless you violate some of their rules, there's no problem in it. Make it free, get feedback from users, fix bugs, and upload updates.

You can use recipes from this book without any limitations, but don't forget that programming is more of an art than a science. Modify the code for yourself; *make it yours*. While it's still better to read from beginning to end, it's not a requirement. Be creative, find the recipes you need now, and use them. It's important that you understand what you use, and for this reason, each recipe has an explanation.

If you're an experienced developer, you can simply pick code snippets from GitHub. You know what to do. If something doesn't work for you or you know a better way of implementing a feature, send your feedback to swiftrecipes@foxicorn.com. It will be highly appreciated!

Good Code

The purpose of this book is to give you good code snippets that you can use in your projects or modify for your own needs. But what is *good* code and what's the difference between *good* and *bad* code?

Let's imagine that you have a function that compiles, doesn't generate errors or warnings, and works perfectly well in production. Is that good code?

```swift
func f1(aaa: Int) -> Int {
    var bbb: Int? = aaa
    bbb = bbb! + 1
    return bbb!
}
```

What is this code about? If you know Swift, you'll figure out that it's a simple increment function. But it looks ugly... so we can say that this is bad code. Programming is beautiful!

```swift
func inc(i: Int) -> Int {
    i + 1
}
```

Looking at the second code snippet, a programmer (including yourself) will tell what it is instantly. And that it will work faster and consume less memory as well. Swift may optimize the first function to work without temporary variables, but it will remain a bad code nonetheless.

Good code must

- Do the work it's supposed to do for all types of arguments. If arguments are not valid for the function, it must be handled correctly.

- Never cause crashes or other critical situations. If the code can't work, it must throw an exception or return nil.

- Use as little code as necessary to do its function. Use language constructs only when they make sense.

- Have names of functions, types, and variables explaining their purpose. Must be readable and understandable by other developers and by yourself if you look at it a year later.

- Use the minimum required system resources: calculation power, memory, disk space, and network.

- Be testable. Each function should do one task, and it must be covered with tests.

As you can see, even though the first code snippet works, it's not readable, it's not optimal, it uses an unnecessary optional variable.... For such a small function, it may not be critical, but if the function was at least 15–20 lines long, it would end up being nonunderstandable code, and you would end up rewriting it instead of reusing it when you need it in the future.

Well-written code doesn't require many comments. Sometimes, comments are necessary, but the code should be as self-explanatory as possible. If the code is understandable for other programmers without comments, it's probably well-written code.

What we called *good* code here is often called *clean* code. There are more principles that make your code even *better* (and often have funny names):

- DRY (Don't Repeat Yourself). Each function is written once and called from different parts of the code. If the code is not DRY, it's WET (Write Every Time, We Enjoy Typing, Waste Everyone's Time).

- Two or more, use a for. This rule means that you shouldn't write the same line of code twice, giving preference to a loop.

- SoC (Separation of Concerns). This design principle offers to do only one task in each code fragment (function, method, or even class).

The recipes offered in the following chapters strictly follow these principles.

NS or Not NS

Many recipes will use the `String` and `Data` types. But there are `NSString` and `NSData` as well. What's the difference between them, and what NS even means?

The prefix NS comes from NeXT company and its platform NeXTSTEP. They made personal computers and wrote software for them. Sounds familiar, doesn't it?

In 1997, Apple acquired NeXT and created a new operating system, MacOS X, which we know now as macOS. This operating system was supposed to replace MacOS 9 on Apple computers, and in 2001, that's exactly what happened. Mac OS X was built on the same Mach kernel as NeXTSTEP, and it was much closer to NeXTSTEP than to Mac OS 9.

The main programming language in NeXTSTEP, and later MacOS X, was Objective-C. If C++ was designed as "C with classes," Objective-C was "C with messages." This language was developed independently from Apple or NeXTSTEP, but shortly after NeXT wrote an extension to GCC compiler to support Objective-C and developed two frameworks: Application Kit and Foundation Kit. That's where the prefix NS appeared.

Application Kit (AppKit) is used in macOS development up to the present day, known as Cocoa. Foundation is used in iOS, watchOS, iPadOS, tvOS, and macOS platforms. UIKit (also known as Cocoa Touch) is the mobile adaptation of Application Kit.

What's the difference between types starting with NS and without it? Having types inherited from the NeXTSTEP platform, Objective-C kept it up to the present day. But when Apple introduced Swift, they introduced new, redesigned types: String, Data, and others. This allowed them to remove unnecessary methods from these classes and to add new ones. Unlike Swift, Objective-C is backward compatible, which means that many methods of standard types were written in the 1980s.

At the same time, Swift is fully compatible with Objective-C and inherits all of its types. That's why you have both String and NSString, Data and NSData, Array and NSArray, and so on. It's always better to use native Swift types, without the NS prefix. But when it's necessary, you can cast one type to another. For example:

```
let nsData = NSData()
let data = nsData as Data
```

This cast is not optional, meaning it always succeeds. It's not the same class and not exactly a wrapper, but Apple made it this way. They call it *bridging*. Data has a buffer of bytes and some methods; NSData has a buffer of bytes and some other (partially, the same) methods. That's why this casting is always possible. The inner structure is rather similar. Swift's Array is bridged to Foundation's NSArray, String is bridged to NSString, etc.

Frameworks

Swift uses a system of frameworks to include external code into your project. There are two standard frameworks, and we'll assume that they're included by default:

```
import Foundation
import UIKit
```

If you try some of the examples and see that they don't compile, make sure you include these two frameworks. Usually, when you create a new file, one of them will be already imported.

Note If you import the UIKit framework, you don't need to import Foundation, it happens automatically.

If code uses another framework, it will be imported explicitly. `import` statement will be a part of code snippet.

Apple offers a good number of frameworks "out of the box." They are

- AVFoundation – Framework for playing audio and video files and streams

- CoreData – Framework for storing and accessing data

- WidgetKit – Framework for writing widgets

- ARKit – Augmented reality framework

- MLKit – Machine learning framework

- CoreLocation – Framework giving access to device location

- CryptoKit – Cryptographic framework

- And dozens of other frameworks

These frameworks can be added to the project directly; they have requirements, like iOS version or device capabilities, so some of them must be used with conditions. But including them into the project and importing from iOS code is straightforward.

There are also many third-party frameworks. You can include them directly if you have source code, its compiled version, but the more common way is to use dependency managers. Swift Package Manager (SPM) is integrated into Xcode. It's an official dependency manager introduced in Swift 3.0, but historically the most popular is CocoaPods. It appeared earlier, and most open source libraries support it.

Besides wide support and popularity, CocoaPods has better compatibility with all types of Xcode projects. For example, projects with frameworks and custom schemes experience troubles building with SPM, while CocoaPods handles this situation correctly.

If you don't want to set up CocoaPods, you can always use alternative methods, like SPM or including source code directly into your project. Adding dependency with SPM can be done directly from Xcode, using menu File ➤ Add Packages....

CocoaPods can be initialized with the command pod init. You need to type this command in the terminal in the project root folder. If you don't have CocoaPods installed, you can get instructions on the Official CocoaPods website – `https://cocoapods.org`.

Note   CocoaPods may not directly work on Macs with Apple chips (M1 and others). To run pod commands on Apple processors, add arch -x86_64 before any command.

CocoaPods creates a configuration file – Podfile. In order to use it with Swift, you may want to add this line:

```
use_frameworks!
```

It will make a framework from each dependency, which makes usage in Swift more comfortable. All libraries, even written in Objective-C, can be imported with the `import` statement.

Another possible line is

```
inhibit_all_warnings!
```

This line removes all the warnings from libraries added with CocoaPods. This is not compulsory; even more, in some cases, it can be harmful, so use it with caution. On the other hand, you can't modify source code of external libraries imported with CocoaPods, and you may not like to see warnings you can't fix in Xcode. If you decided to use it after all, it's better to make at least one build without this flag to see if there are any important warnings. If there are, you may want to change it to another library or update the library version.

Another section describes targets and their dependencies. Each target can have a separate set of dependencies. Each dependency is added with the pod statement:

```
target 'MyApp' do
    pod 'Alamofire'
end
```

You can add a version number:

```
target 'MyApp' do
    pod 'Alamofire', '~> 5.0.0'
End
```

This can be useful if the last version is not compatible with your code. By default, the last compatible versions of all libraries will be downloaded.

Compatibility is calculated based on platform. To get the maximum out of external libraries, you need to specify the same platform as your app, for example:

```
platform :ios, '12.0'
```

Every time one of the recipes uses an external library, the pod name will be provided.

Example of a complete Podfile:

```
platform :ios, '12.0'
use_frameworks!
inhibit_all_warnings!

target 'MyApp` do
    # HTTP libraries
    pod 'Alamofire'
  pod 'Kingfisher'
```

```
  # Firebase libraries
  pod 'Firebase/Analytics'
  pod 'Firebase/Crashlytics'
end
```

Swift Versions and Compatibility

Unlike Objective-C, Swift is not backward compatible. Code written
in Swift 1.0 may not be compiled by Swift 2.0 and very likely won't be
compiled by Swift 5.0. At the same time, Swift 5.0 code may use language
features not available in Swift 4.0.

Note   Different versions of Objective-C are not 100% compatible
either, but there were only two major versions of it in the past 37
years. All code used in iOS apps is written in Objective-C 2.0.

At the same time, basic language elements are the same, so the code
will either work or work with little modifications on another version
of Swift.

All code in this book was compiled with Swift 5.5, which is the latest at
the moment of writing these code recipes. Yet, this code should compile on
all 5.x versions of Swift, and most of the recipes even on 4.x versions.

CHAPTER 1

Working with Data

Data processing is a core feature of all computing devices. And iPhones are mobile computers. Your profile on social networks, cookies on websites, emails and SMS messages, even user interfaces – all of them are data structures. For example, iOS storyboards have an XML format; you can open them in a text editor.

That's why it's important to learn how to handle data as a starting point. We will work with the `Data` class representing binary data; we will convert data types and handle conversion errors, extract data from `Dictionary` and `Array` (which are Swift representations of XML, JSON, and other interchange formats), and we will create these structures to pass data to APIs. In the end, we'll talk about serialization and deserialization, which are extremely important concepts in data processing.

Conversion Between Data Types

All programming languages have basic data types and more complex structures – and Swift is not an exception. The basic types in Swift are as follows:

- `Int` – An integer number. For example, 1, 15, or -1536. Depending on the architecture, it can be a 32-bit or a 64-bit number. All modern Apple devices have 64-bit processors. On these platforms, the Int range goes from -2^{63} to $2^{63} - 1$. If you need to use a bigger or

© Alexander Nekrasov 2022
A. Nekrasov, *Swift Recipes for iOS Developers*,
https://doi.org/10.1007/978-1-4842-8098-0_1

smaller range, you can add a width integer (the amount of memory bits needed to store a value) to the type name. Examples are Int16 and Int64. Unsigned integers have the UInt type.

- Float and Double – A floating-point number, 32-bit and 64-bit, respectively. These types are actively used in UI development. All coordinates on the screen are floating points. Float range is $1.2 * 10^{-38}$ to $3.4 * 10^{38}$. Double range is $2.3 * 10^{-308}$ to $1.7 * 10^{308}$. An example of a floating-point number is 3.14159265359.

- Bool – A Boolean value, which can take only one of two values: true or false. Used for logical expressions and storing simple values (yes/no).

- String – Textual data. In Swift, it's a Unicode text string, which means it may contain text in all languages and even emojis.

- Character – One character. In Swift, it's a 16-bit value.

Besides the basic types, there are hundreds of more complex types, which are structures containing basic types or other structures.

What do we mean by data conversion? Swift is a strictly typed language, and while languages like C or JavaScript allow scenarios like this: a = 1 if (a) ..., in Swift, it's not acceptable. You can use Boolean variables only inside an if statement, and you can only assign Double value to Double variables, not even to the Float ones. It helps to avoid many mistakes but forces developers to perform data conversion manually. There are more complex examples of data conversion. For example, 1 and "1" are not the same thing, even though it may seem so at first glance. The first case is an integer value, while the second one is a text (String or

Character). To convert one type to another, you need to write additional code. And it's important not to forget about possible problems. What if the value in a String is too big for Int? What if it's not a number? What if it's "1", true or false?

Safe Number Conversion

If you have several different number types, for example, Int and Double, you can convert them this way:

```
let d: Double = 1.0
let i = Int(d)
```

In the preceding example, the variable i will have the value 1. If the value of d doesn't fit the range of i, you'll get... a crash:

```
let d: Double = 1000000000.0
let i = Int16(d)
```

Output: Fatal error: Double value cannot be converted to Int16 because the result would be greater than Int16.max.

The solution is to use optional constructor init?(exactly:):

```
let d: Double = 1000000000.0
let i = Int16(exactly: d)
```

The variable i will be optional and will have the Int16? type, and instead of crashing the app, it will become nil. There's one serious problem left – init?(exactly:) returns a non-nil value only if the floating-point value doesn't have fractional parts. If d is 10.5, the conversion will return `nil`. This problem has a beautiful solution - the `rounded()` method. It solves two problems:

- It allows exact conversions – `10.9` won't return `nil` anymore.

- It rounds numbers following mathematical rules. For example, `10.9` will become `11`.

If rounding is not a desired behavior, there's another option – the floor function. For example:

```
var i = Int16(exactly: trunk(d))
```

Finally, let's make it even more universal and allow `d` to be optional:

```
extension Double {
    var asInt16: Int16? {
        Int16(exactly: self.rounded())
    }
}

let d1: Double? = 1000000000.0
let d2: Double? = 10.9
let i1 = d1?.asInt16     // nil
let i2 = d2?.asInt16     // 11
```

In Recipe 1-1, we make an extension of the `Double` class. It automatically works on `Double?`. It's simple, 100% safe, and universal.

Recipe 1-1. Safe Numeric Conversions

```
public extension Int8 {
    var asInt16: Int16 {
        Int16(self)
    }
```

```swift
var asInt32: Int32 {
    Int32(self)
}

var asInt64: Int64 {
    Int64(self)
}

var asInt: Int {
    Int(self)
}

var asUInt8: UInt8? {
    UInt8(exactly: self)
}

var asUInt16: UInt16? {
    UInt16(exactly: self)
}

var asUInt32: UInt32? {
    UInt32(exactly: self)
}

var asUInt64: UInt64? {
    UInt64(exactly: self)
}

var asUInt: UInt? {
    UInt(exactly: self)
}

var asFloat: Float {
    Float(self)
}
```

```
    var asDouble: Double {
        Double(self)
    }
}

public extension UInt8 {
    var asInt8: Int8? {
        Int8(exactly: self)
    }

    var asInt16: Int16 {
        Int16(self)
    }

    var asInt32: Int32 {
        Int32(self)
    }

    var asInt64: Int64 {
        Int64(self)
    }

    var asInt: Int {
        Int(self)
    }

    var asUInt16: UInt16 {
        UInt16(self)
    }

    var asUInt32: UInt32 {
        UInt32(self)
    }
```

```swift
    var asUInt64: UInt64 {
        UInt64(self)
    }

    var asUInt: UInt {
        UInt(self)
    }

    var asFloat: Float {
        Float(self)
    }

    var asDouble: Double {
        Double(self)
    }
}
public extension Int16 {
    var asInt8: Int8? {
        Int8(exactly: self)
    }

    var asInt32: Int32 {
        Int32(self)
    }

    var asInt64: Int64 {
        Int64(self)
    }

    var asInt: Int {
        Int(self)
    }
```

```swift
    var asUInt8: UInt8? {
        UInt8(exactly: self)
    }

    var asUInt16: UInt16? {
        UInt16(exactly: self)
    }

    var asUInt32: UInt32? {
        UInt32(exactly: self)
    }

    var asUInt64: UInt64? {
        UInt64(exactly: self)
    }

    var asUInt: UInt? {
        UInt(exactly: self)
    }

    var asFloat: Float {
        Float(self)
    }

    var asDouble: Double {
        Double(self)
    }
}

public extension UInt16 {
    var asInt8: Int8? {
        Int8(exactly: self)
    }
```

```
var asInt16: Int16? {
    Int16(exactly: self)
}

var asInt32: Int32 {
    Int32(self)
}

var asInt64: Int64 {
    Int64(self)
}

var asInt: Int {
    Int(self)
}

var asUInt8: UInt8? {
    UInt8(exactly: self)
}

var asUInt32: UInt32 {
    UInt32(self)
}

var asUInt64: UInt64 {
    UInt64(self)
}

var asUInt: UInt {
    UInt(self)
}

var asFloat: Float {
    Float(self)
}
```

```
    var asDouble: Double {
        Double(self)
    }
}

public extension Int32 {
    var asInt8: Int8? {
        Int8(exactly: self)
    }

    var asInt16: Int16? {
        Int16(exactly: self)
    }

    var asInt64: Int64 {
        Int64(self)
    }

    var asInt: Int {
        Int(self)
    }

    var asUInt8: UInt8? {
        UInt8(exactly: self)
    }

    var asUInt16: UInt16? {
        UInt16(exactly: self)
    }

    var asUInt32: UInt32? {
        UInt32(exactly: self)
    }
```

```swift
    var asUInt64: UInt64? {
        UInt64(exactly: self)
    }

    var asUInt: UInt? {
        UInt(exactly: self)
    }

    var asFloat: Float {
        Float(self)
    }

    var asDouble: Double {
        Double(self)
    }
}

public extension UInt32 {
    var asInt8: Int8? {
        Int8(exactly: self)
    }

    var asInt16: Int16? {
        Int16(exactly: self)
    }

    var asInt32: Int32? {
        Int32(exactly: self)
    }

    var asInt64: Int64 {
        Int64(self)
    }
```

```
    var asInt: Int? {
        Int(exactly: self)
    }

    var asUInt8: UInt8? {
        UInt8(exactly: self)
    }

    var asUInt16: UInt16? {
        UInt16(exactly: self)
    }

    var asUInt64: UInt64 {
        UInt64(self)
    }

    var asUInt: UInt {
        UInt(self)
    }

    var asFloat: Float {
        Float(self)
    }

    var asDouble: Double {
        Double(self)
    }
}

public extension Int64 {
    var asInt8: Int8? {
        Int8(exactly: self)
    }
```

```swift
var asInt16: Int16? {
    Int16(exactly: self)
}

var asInt32: Int32? {
    Int32(exactly: self)
}

var asInt: Int? {
    Int(exactly: self)
}

var asUInt8: UInt8? {
    UInt8(exactly: self)
}

var asUInt16: UInt16? {
    UInt16(exactly: self)
}

var asUInt32: UInt32? {
    UInt32(exactly: self)
}

var asUInt64: UInt64? {
    UInt64(exactly: self)
}

var asUInt: UInt? {
    UInt(exactly: self)
}

var asFloat: Float {
    Float(self)
}
```

```swift
    var asDouble: Double {
        Double(self)
    }
}

public extension UInt64 {
    var asInt8: Int8? {
        Int8(exactly: self)
    }

    var asInt16: Int16? {
        Int16(exactly: self)
    }

    var asInt32: Int32? {
        Int32(exactly: self)
    }

    var asInt64: Int64? {
        Int64(exactly: self)
    }

    var asInt: Int? {
        Int(exactly: self)
    }

    var asUInt8: UInt8? {
        UInt8(exactly: self)
    }

    var asUInt16: UInt16? {
        UInt16(exactly: self)
    }
```

```
    var asUInt32: UInt32? {
        UInt32(exactly: self)
    }

    var asUInt: UInt? {
        UInt(exactly: self)
    }

    var asFloat: Float {
        Float(self)
    }

    var asDouble: Double {
        Double(self)
    }
}

public extension Int {
    var asInt8: Int8? {
        Int8(exactly: self)
    }

    var asInt16: Int16? {
        Int16(exactly: self)
    }

    var asInt32: Int32? {
        Int32(exactly: self)
    }

    var asInt64: Int64 {
        Int64(self)
    }
```

```swift
    var asUInt8: UInt8? {
        UInt8(exactly: self)
    }

    var asUInt16: UInt16? {
        UInt16(exactly: self)
    }

    var asUInt32: UInt32? {
        UInt32(exactly: self)
    }

    var asUInt64: UInt64? {
        UInt64(exactly: self)
    }

    var asUInt: UInt? {
        UInt(exactly: self)
    }

    var asFloat: Float {
        Float(self)
    }

    var asDouble: Double {
        Double(self)
    }
}

public extension UInt {
    var asInt8: Int8? {
        Int8(exactly: self)
    }
```

```
var asInt16: Int16? {
    Int16(exactly: self)
}

var asInt32: Int32? {
    Int32(exactly: self)
}

var asInt64: Int64? {
    Int64(exactly: self)
}

var asInt: Int? {
    Int(exactly: self)
}

var asUInt8: UInt8? {
    UInt8(exactly: self)
}

var asUInt16: UInt16? {
    UInt16(exactly: self)
}

var asUInt32: UInt32? {
    UInt32(exactly: self)
}

var asUInt64: UInt64 {
    UInt64(self)
}

var asFloat: Float {
    Float(self)
}
```

```
    var asDouble: Double {
        Double(self)
    }
}

public extension Float {
    var asInt8: Int8? {
        Int8(exactly: self.rounded())
    }

    var asInt16: Int16? {
        Int16(exactly: self.rounded())
    }

    var asInt32: Int32? {
        Int32(exactly: self.rounded())
    }

    var asInt64: Int64? {
        Int64(exactly: self.rounded())
    }

    var asInt: Int? {
        Int(exactly: self.rounded())
    }

    var asUInt8: UInt8? {
        UInt8(exactly: self.rounded())
    }

    var asUInt16: UInt16? {
        UInt16(exactly: self.rounded())
    }
```

```
    var asUInt32: UInt32? {
        UInt32(exactly: self.rounded())
    }

    var asUInt64: UInt64? {
        UInt64(exactly: self.rounded())
    }

    var asUInt: UInt? {
        UInt(exactly: self.rounded())
    }

    var asDouble: Double {
        Double(self)
    }
}

public extension Double {
    var asInt8: Int8? {
        Int8(exactly: self.rounded())
    }

    var asInt16: Int16? {
        Int16(exactly: self.rounded())
    }

    var asInt32: Int32? {
        Int32(exactly: self.rounded())
    }

    var asInt64: Int64? {
        Int64(exactly: self.rounded())
    }
```

```swift
    var asInt: Int? {
        Int(exactly: self.rounded())
    }

    var asUInt8: UInt8? {
        UInt8(exactly: self.rounded())
    }

    var asUInt16: UInt16? {
        UInt16(exactly: self.rounded())
    }

    var asUInt32: UInt32? {
        UInt32(exactly: self.rounded())
    }

    var asUInt64: UInt64? {
        UInt64(exactly: self.rounded())
    }

    var asUInt: UInt? {
        UInt(exactly: self.rounded())
    }

    var asFloat: Float? {
        Float(exactly: self)
    }
}
```

This recipe allows you to safely convert one numeric type to another as well as chaining such conversions. For example, if you have an `Int`, but function is presented as `Double` extension, this chaining solves the problem: `x.asDouble.process.asInt`.

Note   The best way to learn is to try. And the best way to try Swift code is Xcode Playground (Figure 1-1). To create a new playground, open Xcode, open File menu, choose New and Playground....

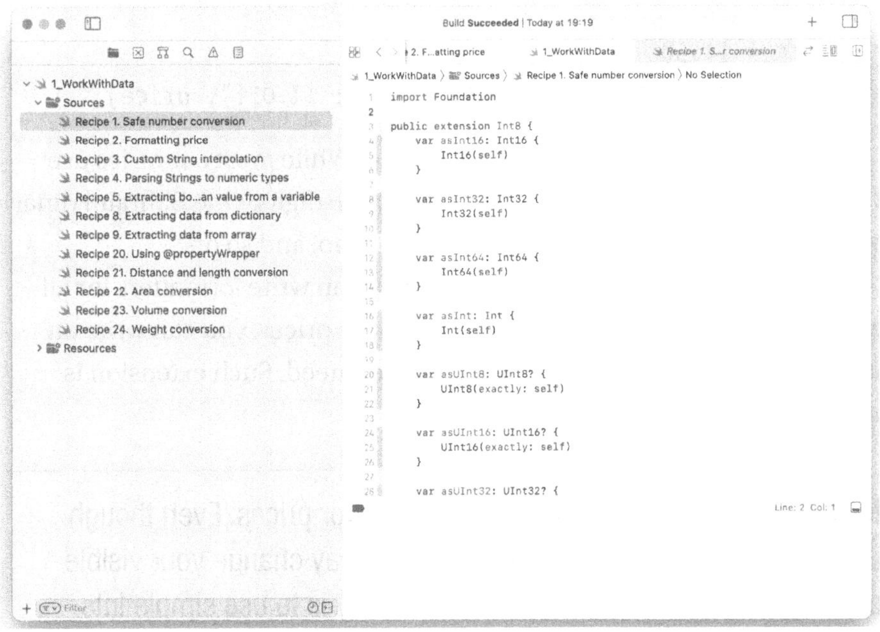

Figure 1-1. *Swift Playground*

Conversion from Number to String and Back

The easiest way to convert numbers of any type to a String is a *string interpolation*. In Swift, you can include any variable inside a String by adding \(before a variable name and) after. It works even with expressions and functions. For example:

```
let age = 30
let str = "Your age is \(age). Next year you'll be \(age+1)"
```

It's more complicated if you need to format it. If you need to get a string with a price, you probably want to have two digits for the monetary part.

There are two ways. You can use the `String(format:_:...)` constructor. The first argument is a template; others are variables. If you are familiar with the C-family programming languages, you know the `sprintf` function. It works exactly the same way. Example:

```
let price = 14.50
let priceString = String(format: "Price: $%.02f", price)
```

Sometimes, you need to be more flexible. While most countries use two digits for monetary units, others need three digits. One Bahraini dinar equals 1000 fils, one Chinese yuan equals 10 jiao, and so on.

Depending on the app functionality, you can write formatters for all necessary data types. If you use `Double` to store prices, you can write an extension to format it and use it wherever you need. Such extension is shown in Recipe 1-2.

Note   It's not a good idea to use `Double` for prices. Even though they have high precision, losing 0.000...1 may change your visible price from 1.00 to 0.99. A more reliable way is to use simple Ints and keep prices in monetary units. Alternatively, you can use more complex data structures storing as two `Int` variables – for full units and monetary units.

Recipe 1-2. Formatting Price

```
public extension Double {
    var asPrice: String {
        guard let cents = (self * 100.0).asInt else {
            return ""
        }
```

```
        return String(format: "%d.%02d", cents / 100, cents % 100)
    }
}

public extension Int {
    var asPrice: String {
        String(format: "%d.%02d", self / 100, self % 100)
    }
}
```

Usage

```
let price = 14.5
let priceString = "Price: $\(price.asPrice)"
```

Similarly, you can format any other data.

Another way to format numbers is extending `String.`
`StringInterpolation`. It gives you access to interpolation logic. Typically, it's used for dates and custom types, but you can use it for numbers as well. Unless the app has scientific purposes, you won't need more than three decimals for doubles.

The fast solution is the following:

```
public extension String.StringInterpolation {
    mutating func appendInterpolation(_ value: Double) {
        let formatter = NumberFormatter()
        formatter.decimalSeparator = "."
        formatter.maximumFractionDigits = 3

        if let result = formatter.string(from: value as NSNumber) {
            appendLiteral(result)
        }
    }
}
```

The preceding extension limits the amount of fraction digits to three and adds decimal separators.

But it's fast only to write when you use it in UITableView or UICollectionView; it may cause performance issues. Why? Because we create and set up NumberFormatter every time.

The correct solution is to create a lazy variable, which will create our NumberFormatter once, and then reuse it every time. We can't create variables in extensions, so we'll have to create a helper class as shown in Recipe 1-3.

Recipe 1-3. Custom String Interpolation

```
class MyFormatters {
    static var formatterWithThreeFractionDigits:
    NumberFormatter = {
        let formatter = NumberFormatter()
        formatter.decimalSeparator = "."
        formatter.maximumFractionDigits = 3
        return formatter
    }()
}

public extension String.StringInterpolation {
    mutating func appendInterpolation(_ value: Double) {
        let formatter = MyFormatters.
        formatterWithThreeFractionDigits
        if let result = formatter.string(from: value as
        NSNumber) {
            appendLiteral(result)
        }
    }
}
```

Note   All static variables are lazy, so you don't have to add lazy keyword. Even more, you can't do it.

What about the opposite conversion? If we get a `String`, how can we convert it to `Int` or `Double` to perform numeric operations? A simple answer is

```
let str = "123.5"
let i = Int(str)
let d = Double(str)
```

This code is safe because it returns optionals. i in the preceding example will be `nil`, while d will be `123.5`. It's a really good working code, but there are two problematic situations:

1. If str is optional, it won't compile. This can be solved with a nil-coalescing operator (`str ?? ""`). If str is `nil`, it will be replaced with an empty string. As empty strings can't be parsed as a number (neither Double nor Int), the result will be `nil`.

2. In some locales, decimal separator is "," instead of ".". This can be a problem when we parse user input. A quick fix is replacing commas with dots: `.replacingOccurrences(of: ",", with: ".")`.

Let's wrap it up and make an easy-to-use `String` extension (Recipe 1-4).

Recipe 1-4. Parsing Strings to Numeric Types

```
public extension StringProtocol {
    var asInt8: Int8? {
        Int8(self)
    }
}
```

25

```
var asUInt8: UInt8? {
    UInt8(self)
}

var asInt16: Int16? {
    Int16(self)
}

var asUInt16: UInt16? {
    UInt16(self)
}

var asInt32: Int32? {
    Int32(self)
}

var asUInt32: UInt32? {
    UInt32(self)
}

var asInt64: Int64? {
    Int64(self)
}

var asUInt64: UInt64? {
    UInt64(self)
}

var asInt: Int? {
    Int(self)
}
```

```swift
    var asUInt: UInt? {
        UInt(self)
    }

    var asDouble: Double? {
        Double(self.replacingOccurrences(of: ",", with: "."))
    }

    var asFloat: Float? {
        Float(self.replacingOccurrences(of: ",", with: "."))
    }
}
```

Boolean Conversions

Even though Bool is the simplest type with only two values, parsing it can be a challenge. To understand why, try to figure out if 1 is true or false. Most developers will say that 1 is undoubtedly true because 0 is false and any other value is true. This is how it works under the hood in Swift and most other programming languages. In some cases, 0 may mean success (no error), and other values – error code. Keep it in mind if you have such case, but we'll assume that Int should convert to false if it's 0, and to true otherwise .

Other questions are if "yes" or "true" should be parsed as true and what to do with custom values like 5 or "success". It depends on the source of the data. You should read the documentation of the API or library you use and decide accordingly.

Recipe 1-5 follows the set of rules specified in Table 1-1.

Table 1-1. *Any to Bool conversion rules*

Parsed type	Rules
Bool	Return parsed value as is.
Int	Return `false` if the value is 0, otherwise `true`.
Float or Double	Return `nil` to avoid confusion. Booleans should never be represented as floating-point numbers.
String	Return `true` if the value is "true" or "yes"; return `false` if the value is "false" or "no"; return `nil` in all other cases. String comparison should be case-insensitive.
Other types	Return `nil`.

Recipe 1-5. Extracting Boolean Value from a Variable

```swift
// Any can't be extended, so it's a function
func parseAsBool(value: Any?) -> Bool? {
    if let boolValue = value as? Bool {
        return boolValue
    } else if let intValue = value as? Int {
        return intValue != 0
    } else if value is Float || value is Double {
        return nil
    } else if let strValue = value as? String {
        let strPrepared = strValue.trimmingCharacters(in:
        .whitespacesAndNewlines).lowercased()
        if strPrepared == "true" || strPrepared == "yes" {
            return true
        } else if strPrepared == "false" || strPrepared
        == "no" {
            return false
```

```
        } else {
            return nil
        }
    } else {
        return nil
    }
}
```

If you prefer all numeric types to be converted to Bool, you can use the isZero function instead of returning nil. If Double.isZero returns true, you return false. Otherwise, you return true.

String to Data and Back

String and Data are highly used types in Swift. Data has a buffer of bytes without any particular semantics. String is basically the same, but Swift interprets this buffer as a sequence of characters, including special symbols, such as spaces and newlines.

Depending on the use case, you may need to turn String to Data or vice versa.

```
let data = Data()
let str = String(data: data, encoding: .utf8)
```

If data can't be parsed using specified encoding (UTF-8 in this case), this code will return nil. For example, if you read a JPEG file from an iPhone storage (or download it from the Internet) and send it to a String constructor, it will always return nil.

The conversion from String to Data rarely fails with UTF-8 encoding:

```
let str = "I'm a string"
let data = str.data(using: .utf8)
```

But potentially you may need to get it encoded into ASCII (American Standard Code for Information Interchange), which was the standard before UTF was introduced. ASCII uses 7 bits per symbol and supports only 128 characters, including special ones. Arabic, Japanese, or Cyrillic symbols can't be encoded this way, so the conversion will fail. Data will be nil. Conversion of UTF8 data is shown in Recipe 1-6.

We will discuss the String type and its features in more details in the second chapter.

Recipe 1-6. Conversion Between String and Data

```
public extension StringProtocol {
    var asUtf8Data: Data {
        data(using: .utf8)!
    }
}

public extension Data {
    var asUtf8String: String? {
        String(data: self, encoding: .utf8)
    }
}
```

Dates, Timestamps, and ISO 8601 Format

We often need to represent dates as a string. Swift has an integrated Date structure. It represents both date and time, it supports time zones, and it's used as an argument or return type in many functions and methods. The biggest problem of using Date is that it's an internal Swift format – you can't pass it to a server; you have to convert it to a String, Int, or another universal format.

One of the standards is called *Timestamp* or *UNIX Timestamp*. It's an integer value, indicating the amount of seconds or milliseconds since *epoch.* Epoch is the midnight of January 1, 1970. In Swift, timestamps are represented as Double; they have an integer part (seconds) and a fractional part (fractions of seconds).

These two functions – one method and one constructor – convert Date to Double and back:

```
let date = Date()
let timestamp = date.timeIntervalSince1970
let restoredDate = Date(timeIntervalSince1970: timestamp)
```

The biggest problem in timestamps is the lack of information about time zones. Swift Date returns the amount of seconds since January 1, 1970, UTC (Coordinated Universal Time). So if you convert it to a Date object, you need to make correct time zone conversion.

Another way to represent time is the ISO 8601 format. ISO stands for International Organization for Standardization. Everything starting with ISO means that it's a standard.

Swift doesn't offer a conversion option between ISO 8601 String and Date out of the box, but it's rather easy to implement it using the DateFormatter class as shown in Recipe 1-7.

Recipe 1-7. Date to ISO 8601

```
public extension Formatter {
    static let iso8601withFractionalSeconds: DateFormatter = {
        let formatter = DateFormatter()
        formatter.calendar = Calendar(identifier: .iso8601)
        formatter.locale = Locale(identifier: "en_US_POSIX")
        formatter.dateFormat = "yyyy-MM-dd'T'HH:mm:ss.SSSZZZZZ"
        return formatter
    }()
}
```

```
public extension Date {
    var iso8601String: String {
        Formatter.iso8601withFractionalSeconds.
        string(from: self)
    }

    init?(iso8601String: String) {
        guard let date = Formatter.
        iso8601withFractionalSeconds.date(from:
        iso8601String) else {
            return nil
        }
        self = date
    }
}
```

Usage

```
let dateWrong = Date(iso8601String: "It's 5 o'clock")
// dateWrong is nil

let dateCorrect = Date(iso8601String:
"2021-07-01T18:30:00.000+04:00")
// dateCorrect is a valid Date object
```

Please note that in a debug session, you'll see time in your local time zone, which is what you usually want to show to the user.

Extracting Data from Dictionaries and Arrays

You can't do much with simple data types. In real-life apps, more complex types are used. You can have a structure containing different data types and different structures inside. It's called Dictionary. Basically, a Dictionary is a set of keys and values. They can be limited with particular data types. You'll rarely see the keyword `Dictionary` in Swift code. A more common syntax is

```
var dict: [String: Any] = [:]
```

This code created a `Dictionary` variable. Each key must be a `String`. The value can have any type, including another dictionary.

In case if you need an ordered list of values of the same type, you can use an `Array`. It doesn't have keys but uses indexes instead.

```
var arr: [String] = []
```

Complex Data Types

The composition of dictionaries and arrays allows you to create data structures of any complexity.

It's easy to spot the similarity with JSON (JavaScript Object Notation) structures. JSON is the most popular format for API requests and responses. When a mobile app requests a reading of the weather forecast, user info, or any other data from the server, it's almost guaranteed it gets JSON.

Parsing JSON structures from `String` or `Data` returned by API will be discussed later. Let's focus on extracting data from `Dictionary` and `Array` now.

Extracting Data from Dictionary

Let's say we have a `Dictionary`:

```
var dict: [String: Any] = [
  "name": "John",
  "surname": "Doe",
  "age": 30
]
```

It's John's birthday, so we need to make him one year older:

```
if var age = dict["age"] {
  age += 1
  dict["age"] = age
}
```

And here we have a problem – the code won't compile. age is not a number; it's Any. We can't increment Any; it doesn't make sense. Type casting could solve the problem:

```
if var age = dict["age"] as? Int {
  age += 1
  dict["age"] = age
}
```

And this is a working code, except for one situation. API responses are usually generated by scripting, not strictly typed languages, like JavaScript. There's a big chance that age will be "30" instead of 30. The opposite problem is also possible. If the text string consists of digits, it can be parsed as a number. For example, a bank card number can be parsed as a big Int, and you may need it as a String. Or user's password 123456 can be parsed as an Int instead of String.

As we already know, Swift type casting doesn't turn Int into String automatically. And Bool variables are completely uncertain. Dictionary extension from Recipe 1-8 will help us to solve this problem.

Recipe 1-8. Extracting Data from Dictionary

```
public extension Dictionary where Key:
ExpressibleByStringLiteral {
    func getInt8(_ key: String, defVal: Int8? = nil) -> Int8? {
        let val = self[key as! Key]
        if val == nil {
```

```
        return defVal
    }

    if let ival = val as? Int8 {
        return ival
    }

    if let dval = val as? Double {
        return dval.asInt8
    }

    if let sval = val as? String {
        return sval.asInt8 ?? defVal
    }

    return defVal
}
func getUInt8(_ key: String, defVal: UInt8? = nil) -> UInt8? {
    let val = self[key as! Key]
    if val == nil {
        return defVal
    }

    if let ival = val as? UInt8 {
        return ival
    }

    if let dval = val as? Double {
        return dval.asUInt8
    }

    if let sval = val as? String {
        return sval.asUInt8 ?? defVal
    }
```

```
            return defVal
    }

    func getInt16(_ key: String, defVal: Int16? = nil) ->
    Int16? {
        let val = self[key as! Key]
        if val == nil {
            return defVal
        }

        if let ival = val as? Int16 {
            return ival
        }

        if let dval = val as? Double {
            return dval.asInt16
        }

        if let sval = val as? String {
            return sval.asInt16 ?? defVal
        }

        return defVal
    }

    func getUInt16(_ key: String, defVal: UInt16? = nil) ->
    UInt16? {
        let val = self[key as! Key]
        if val == nil {
            return defVal
        }

        if let ival = val as? UInt16 {
            return ival
        }
```

```
    if let dval = val as? Double {
        return dval.asUInt16
    }

    if let sval = val as? String {
        return sval.asUInt16 ?? defVal
    }

    return defVal
}
func getInt32(_ key: String, defVal: Int32? = nil) ->
Int32? {
    let val = self[key as! Key]
    if val == nil {
        return defVal
    }

    if let ival = val as? Int32 {
        return ival
    }

    if let dval = val as? Double {
        return dval.asInt32
    }

    if let sval = val as? String {
        return sval.asInt32 ?? defVal
    }

    return defVal
}
func getUInt32(_ key: String, defVal: UInt32? = nil) ->
UInt32? {
```

```
        let val = self[key as! Key]
        if val == nil {
            return defVal
        }

        if let ival = val as? UInt32 {
            return ival
        }

        if let dval = val as? Double {
            return dval.asUInt32
        }

        if let sval = val as? String {
            return sval.asUInt32 ?? defVal
        }

        return defVal
    }

    func getInt64(_ key: String, defVal: Int64? = nil) ->
    Int64? {
        let val = self[key as! Key]
        if val == nil {
            return defVal
        }

        if let ival = val as? Int64 {
            return ival
        }

        if let dval = val as? Double {
            return dval.asInt64
        }
```

```
    if let sval = val as? String {
        return sval.asInt64 ?? defVal
    }

    return defVal
}

func getUInt64(_ key: String, defVal: UInt64? = nil) ->
UInt64? {
    let val = self[key as! Key]
    if val == nil {
        return defVal
    }

    if let ival = val as? UInt64 {
        return ival
    }

    if let dval = val as? Double {
        return dval.asUInt64
    }

    if let sval = val as? String {
        return sval.asUInt64 ?? defVal
    }

    return defVal
}

func getInt(_ key: String, defVal: Int? = nil) -> Int? {
    let val = self[key as! Key]
    if val == nil {
        return defVal
    }
```

```
    if let ival = val as? Int {
        return ival
    }

    if let dval = val as? Double {
        return dval.asInt
    }

    if let sval = val as? String {
        return sval.asInt ?? defVal
    }

    return defVal
}

func geUtInt(_ key: String, defVal: UInt? = nil) -> UInt? {
    let val = self[key as! Key]
    if val == nil {
        return defVal
    }

    if let ival = val as? UInt {
        return ival
    }

    if let dval = val as? Double {
        return dval.asUInt
    }

    if let sval = val as? String {
        return sval.asUInt ?? defVal
    }

    return defVal
}
```

```swift
func getFloat(_ key: String, defVal: Float? = nil) ->
Float? {
    let val = self[key as! Key]
    if val == nil {
        return defVal
    }

    if let fval = val as? Float {
        return fval
    }

    if let ival = val as? Int {
        return ival.asFloat
    }

    if let sval = val as? String {
        return sval.asFloat ?? defVal
    }

    return defVal
}
func getDouble(_ key: String, defVal: Double? = nil) ->
Double? {
    let val = self[key as! Key]
    if val == nil {
        return defVal
    }

    if let dval = val as? Double {
        return dval
    }

    if let ival = val as? Int {
        return ival.asDouble
```

```swift
        }

        if let sval = val as? String {
            return sval.asDouble ?? defVal
        }

        return defVal
    }

    func getString(_ key: String, defVal: String? = nil) ->
    String? {
        let val = self[key as! Key]
        if val == nil {
            return defVal
        }

        if let sval = val as? String {
            return sval.trimmingCharacters(in:
            .whitespacesAndNewlines)
        }

        return defVal
    }

    func getBool(_ key: String, defVal: Bool? = nil) -> Bool? {
        let val = self[key as! Key]
        if val == nil {
            return defVal
        }

        return parseAsBool(value: val) ?? defVal
    }
}
```

Extracting Data from Array

Extracting data from typed Array is straightforward:

```
let arr: [String] = ["one", "two", "three"]
let firstElement = arr[0]
```

It would be better to confirm that there's element 0 though. A more complex task is to get typed data from [Any], and we get this type of Array from the parsers.

The logic is the same as for Dictionary, but we need to check if the element with a given index exists as well. If it doesn't, we return nil. The same as if we have a data type conflict. Recipe 1-9 shows the full Array extension.

Recipe 1-9. Extracting Data from Array

```
public extension Array {
    func getInt8(_ idx: Int, defVal: Int8? = nil) -> Int8? {
        if idx < 0 || idx >= count {
            return nil
        }

        let val = self[idx]

        if let ival = val as? Int8 {
            return ival
        }

        if let dval = val as? Double {
            return dval.asInt8
        }

        if let sval = val as? String {
            return sval.asInt8 ?? defVal
        }
```

```
        return defVal
    }

    func getUInt8(_ idx: Int, defVal: UInt8? = nil) -> UInt8? {
        if idx < 0 || idx >= count {
            return nil
        }

        let val = self[idx]

        if let ival = val as? UInt8 {
            return ival
        }

        if let dval = val as? Double {
            return dval.asUInt8
        }

        if let sval = val as? String {
            return sval.asUInt8 ?? defVal
        }

        return defVal
    }

    func getInt16(_ idx: Int, defVal: Int16? = nil) -> Int16? {
        if idx < 0 || idx >= count {
            return nil
        }

        let val = self[idx]

        if let ival = val as? Int16 {
            return ival
        }
```

```
    if let dval = val as? Double {
        return dval.asInt16
    }

    if let sval = val as? String {
        return sval.asInt16 ?? defVal
    }

    return defVal
}
func getUInt16(_ idx: Int, defVal: UInt16? = nil) ->
UInt16? {
    if idx < 0 || idx >= count {
        return nil
    }

    let val = self[idx]

    if let ival = val as? UInt16 {
        return ival
    }

    if let dval = val as? Double {
        return dval.asUInt16
    }

    if let sval = val as? String {
        return sval.asUInt16 ?? defVal
    }

    return defVal
}
func getInt32(_ idx: Int, defVal: Int32? = nil) -> Int32? {
```

```swift
    if idx < 0 || idx >= count {
        return nil
    }

    let val = self[idx]

    if let ival = val as? Int32 {
        return ival
    }

    if let dval = val as? Double {
        return dval.asInt32
    }

    if let sval = val as? String {
        return sval.asInt32 ?? defVal
    }

    return defVal
}

func getUInt32(_ idx: Int, defVal: UInt32? = nil) -> UInt32? {
    if idx < 0 || idx >= count {
        return nil
    }

    let val = self[idx]

    if let ival = val as? UInt32 {
        return ival
    }

    if let dval = val as? Double {
        return dval.asUInt32
    }
```

```
    if let sval = val as? String {
        return sval.asUInt32 ?? defVal
    }

    return defVal
}

func getInt64(_ idx: Int, defVal: Int64? = nil) -> Int64? {
    if idx < 0 || idx >= count {
        return nil
    }

    let val = self[idx]

    if let ival = val as? Int64 {
        return ival
    }

    if let dval = val as? Double {
        return dval.asInt64
    }

    if let sval = val as? String {
        return sval.asInt64 ?? defVal
    }

    return defVal
}

func getUInt64(_ idx: Int, defVal: UInt64? = nil) -> UInt64? {
    if idx < 0 || idx >= count {
        return nil
    }

    let val = self[idx]
```

```
    if let ival = val as? UInt64 {
        return ival
    }

    if let dval = val as? Double {
        return dval.asUInt64
    }

    if let sval = val as? String {
        return sval.asUInt64 ?? defVal
    }

    return defVal
}

func getInt(_ idx: Int, defVal: Int? = nil) -> Int? {
    if idx < 0 || idx >= count {
        return nil
    }

    let val = self[idx]

    if let ival = val as? Int {
        return ival
    }

    if let dval = val as? Double {
        return dval.asInt
    }

    if let sval = val as? String {
        return sval.asInt ?? defVal
    }

    return defVal
}
```

```
func geUtInt(_ idx: Int, defVal: UInt? = nil) -> UInt? {
    if idx < 0 || idx >= count {
        return nil
    }

    let val = self[idx]

    if let ival = val as? UInt {
        return ival
    }

    if let dval = val as? Double {
        return dval.asUInt
    }

    if let sval = val as? String {
        return sval.asUInt ?? defVal
    }

    return defVal
}

func getFloat(_ idx: Int, defVal: Float? = nil) -> Float? {
    if idx < 0 || idx >= count {
        return nil
    }

    let val = self[idx]

    if let fval = val as? Float {
        return fval
    }

    if let ival = val as? Int {
        return ival.asFloat
    }
```

```swift
        if let sval = val as? String {
            return sval.asFloat ?? defVal
        }

        return defVal
    }

    func getDouble(_ idx: Int, defVal: Double? = nil) ->
    Double? {
        if idx < 0 || idx >= count {
            return nil
        }

        let val = self[idx]

        if let dval = val as? Double {
            return dval
        }

        if let ival = val as? Int {
            return ival.asDouble
        }

        if let sval = val as? String {
            return sval.asDouble ?? defVal
        }

        return defVal
    }

    func getString(_ idx: Int, defVal: String? = nil) ->
    String? {
        if idx < 0 || idx >= count {
            return nil
        }
```

```
        let val = self[idx]

        if let sval = val as? String {
            return sval.trimmingCharacters(in:
            .whitespacesAndNewlines)
        }

        return defVal
    }

    func getBool(_ idx: Int, defVal: Bool? = nil) -> Bool? {
        if idx < 0 || idx >= count {
            return nil
        }

        let val = self[idx]

        return parseAsBool(value: val) ?? defVal
    }
}
```

Summary

In this chapter, we showed that even simple data types require attention, especially when it comes to type conversion and extracting data from complex types like dictionaries and arrays.

In the next chapter, we'll review such concepts as serialization, data exchange, and data semantics, when number is not just a set of bits and bytes, but length, weight, or distance.

CHAPTER 2

Working with JSON and Other Popular Formats

Data in Swift is much more than basic types, arrays, and dictionaries. Also, a mobile app is rarely isolated from the outer world. It makes API requests and processes responses; it exchanges data with cloud services and works with SDKs. Let's see how to work with data exchange and safely convert numbers between different units.

How Devices Exchange Data

Nowadays, it's hard to imagine a computing device without external data interfaces. Even simple electronic devices like a coffee machine and a heater start to get Wi-Fi and Bluetooth interfaces to heat the room for you and make coffee when you come home from the cold streets.

Fortunately for us – mobile developers – we don't need to go deep into Wi-Fi or Bluetooth protocols. There's one universal standard of data exchange, which mobile developers need in order to write almost any app: HTTP.

© Alexander Nekrasov 2022
A. Nekrasov, *Swift Recipes for iOS Developers*,
https://doi.org/10.1007/978-1-4842-8098-0_2

HTTP (Hypertext Transfer Protocol) and HTTPS (the secure version of it) are application-layer protocols of data exchange. They use the client-server model: the client sends a request, and the server returns a response. Format, encoding, and other properties are defined by headers.

The HTTP protocol is so popular that it's often used to communicate within one device. One app becomes the server, and another – the client. To address a server, you need to know the URL (Uniform Resource Locator). It has several components: scheme, host, port, path, arguments, and fragment.

Desktop server apps usually reserve a port for themselves. That's how several servers can coexist within one computer. Mobile apps often reserve a scheme matching their unique app ID. This way, one app can call another, for example, for authentication. Remember signing in with Facebook or Google? It works exactly this way.

When client and server apps establish a connection, they need to exchange data. The data format is defined in headers, and it can have one of the predefined MIME (Multipurpose Internet Mail Extensions) types. If you send a request to the API, you can find the accepted data formats in the pertinent documentation.

The most popular data format for APIs (Application Programming Interfaces) is JSON. Its MIME type is `application/json`. Another possible format is XML – `text/xml`. You may ask why JSON belongs to the application group while XML is text. JSON is JavaScript restricted with data structures, without functions. You can copy-paste or import JSON files to JavaScript apps, and it will read and parse it as JavaScript without any modifications. XML is not source code; it's always data. If XML is not readable by humans and can be only processed by a parser, it can have the `application/xml` MIME type.

To send data to the server as JSON, you should add a header:

```
Content-Type: application/json
```

The server does the same when it responds with JSON. What if you don't include this header in the mobile app? Or what if the server doesn't include it into the response? Depending on the server software, it can accept data and detect JSON automatically, or reject the request as invalid. When the server doesn't include a header, your mobile app can handle it the way it wants. Generally speaking, developers don't want to add unnecessary error messages and make apps more fragile, so if you know that the server is going to respond with JSON, parse it as JSON regardless of headers.

What Are Serialization and Deserialization

Serialization means turning a custom object or data structure into an array of bytes. In Swift, that would be a `Data` object. Serialization to `String` is another option – after all, `String` is a sequence of bytes. We can say that a JSON-formatted `String` is a serialized version of a `Dictionary` or an `Array`.

   Deserialization is a reversed process. It turns an array of bytes into a Swift object.

Working with JSON

As we discussed earlier, JSON is the most popular format for data exchange with APIs. Most SDKs, like Facebook SDK, Firebase SDK, and others, use JSON under the hood. Firestore database and MongoDB have data as JSON (yes, with indexes and other features of a database, but it's still JSON). This makes import, export, and data exchange easy.

Parsing JSON to Dictionary or Array

When you parse JSON using `JSONSerialization` in a Swift app, you get `Any` as a result. The reason of it is uncertainty regarding the data type. JSON has one root element, but it can be an object { ... } or an array [...].

If the root element is an object, Any can be casted to Dictionary, particularly [String: Any]. Otherwise, it's an Array – [Any].

Note   More common way to work with JSON – JSONEncoder/ JSONDecoder. It will be reviewed later in this chapter.

Most networking libraries allow to get data from the server as Data, String, and sometimes as more complex structures. If it's JSON, you need to receive Data even though it's more text. We'll use the Alamofire library, which is the most popular for iOS networking, as an example.

The next step is to turn Data into Any, where Any is either Dictionary or Array. We'll check the data type later, but first, we need to parse it. Swift has a standard JSON parser, which we will use. In case of error, it will throw an exception, so we need to surround it with a do ... try ... catch block. The exception is thrown if the document is not a valid JSON document or if it has data that can't be parsed.

The last step is to check the data type. A JSON document can't be parsed as an Int or a String. It's always either Dictionary or Array. We check if our document has one of these types, and if it doesn't, we return nil. The last scenario should never happen, but we can't be sure that all Swift libraries are bug-free. Full version of this parsing is shown in Recipe 2-1.

Recipe 2-1. Parsing JSON

```
public extension Data {
    var parsedFromJSON: Any? {
        guard let json = try? JSONSerialization.
        jsonObject(with: self, options: .allowFragments) else {
            return nil
        }
```

```swift
        if let jsonDictionary = json as? [String: Any] {
            return jsonDictionary
        } else if let jsonArray = json as? [Any] {
            return jsonArray
        } else {
            return nil
        }
    }

    var parsedAsJSONDictionary: [String: Any]? {
        try? JSONSerialization.jsonObject(with: self, options:
        .allowFragments) as? [String: Any]
    }

    var parsedAsJSONArray: [Any]? {
        try? JSONSerialization.jsonObject(with: self, options:
        .allowFragments) as? [Any]
    }
}

public extension String {
    var parsedFromJSON: Any? {
        asUtf8Data.parsedFromJSON
    }

    var parsedAsJSONDictionary: [String: Any]? {
        asUtf8Data.parsedAsJSONDictionary
    }

    var parsedAsJSONArray: [Any]? {
        asUtf8Data.parsedAsJSONArray
    }
}
```

Generating JSON from Dictionary or Array

The reverse process is even easier as we don't need to check data types or do any other preparations. We convert `Dictionary` or `Array` into `Data` containing JSON and then pass it to the API (or use any other way). This is shown in Recipe 2-2.

There's one thing we need to keep in mind: certain data types can't be converted into JSON. That's the case, for example, if your `Dictionary` has an `UIImage` or `UIView` – it can't be serialized to a JSON element. We'll go deeper into serialization in the next section. We need either to convert them to one of the basic types, to `Dictionary`, or to exclude them from the original structure.

Recipe 2-2. Generating JSON

```
public extension Dictionary where Key:
ExpressibleByStringLiteral {
    var asJSONData: Data? {
        try? JSONSerialization.data(withJSONObject: self,
        options: .fragmentsAllowed)
    }

    var asJSONString: String? {
        asJSONData?.asUtf8String
    }
}

public extension Array {
    var asJSONData: Data? {
        try? JSONSerialization.data(withJSONObject: self,
        options: .fragmentsAllowed)
    }
```

```
    var asJSONString: String? {
        asJSONData?.asUtf8String
    }
}
```

Working with XML

While JSON is popular for data exchange, XML (eXtensible Markup Language) is more commonly used for storing internal app data. Storyboards, nibs, plists, and other structures are based on XML. XML files are used for Android and UWP (Universal Windows Platform) layouts as well.

Some APIs offer a response in XML either as the only option or as one of the possibilities.

Before discussing how to parse XML, it's important to understand that unlike JSON, XML can't be directly converted to Swift Dictionary or Array. JSON is an *object notation*, and `Dictionary` is a way to represent an object, at least it's data. In JavaScript, object is a dictionary.

XML is a *markup language*. It has elements and attributes. These elements and attributes are declared in *schema*. There are namespaces and other constructs that don't exist in Swift dictionaries. But we don't need to go deep into this if we only parse response from API or prepare arguments for an API call. What we need is to extract the data we need.

Parsing XML

Swift offers an internal class XMLParser. It can extract data from XML, but the usage of it is a nightmare. To parse an XML string, you need to declare a delegate, and each XML element (tag) will make a callback:

```
class ParserDelegate: NSObject, XMLParserDelegate {
    func parser(_ parser: XMLParser, didStartElement elementName:
    String, namespaceURI: String?, qualifiedName qName: String?,
    attributes attributeDict: [String : String] = [:]) {
```

```
        print("Found element \(elementName) with attributes \
        (attributeDict)")
    }
}
```

It can be used if we need to get some data, but it's too difficult to get a `Dictionary`.

There's a good helper library: SWXMLHash. It's well maintained, compatible with multiple Swift versions, and available via CocoaPods, Carthage, and Swift Package Manager. If you use CocoaPods, add this to your Podfile:

```
pod 'SWXMLHash'
```

Don't forget to run pod install or pod update.

Now you can parse it with just one line of code:

```
let xmlDict = SWXMLHash.parse(xml)
```

From `xmlDict`, you can extract the data you need. Recipe 2-3 shows the full code.

Recipe 2-3. Parsing XML

```
import SWXMLHash

let xml: String = "<xml>...</xml>"
let xmlDict = SWXMLHash.parse(xml)
```

Generating XML

Generating XML is a very rare task for iOS apps, which we'll discuss for the sake of completeness only. It's unlikely that you'll need to generate XML data and save or send it somewhere. On the other hand, unlikely doesn't mean impossible. You can find the full code in Recipe 2-4. But first, let's see how it works.

As there are no standard solutions and no libraries compatible with the latest Swift version, we'll write a simple XML generator. XML is a recursive structure – a tag can contain other tag, or tags, so this generator will be recursive as well.

We'll divide all elements into three groups:

- Dictionaries

- Arrays

- Basic elements

Array in XML is presented with several tags with the same name, but different content. Dictionary is a tag with tags inside. And a basic element is just a tag with a text string (representing any type) inside.

Basic elements will be generated using the String interpolation that we discussed earlier. For the other two types of elements, we'll use two functions:

Recipe 2-4. Generating XML

```swift
func convertArrayToXML(array: [Any], startElement: String) ->
String {
    var xml = ""
    for value in array {
        if let value = value as? [String: Any] {
            xml += convertDictionaryToXML(dictionary: value,
            startElement: startElement, isFirstElement: false)
        }
        else if let value = value as? [Any] {
            xml += convertArrayToXML(array: value,
            startElement: startElement)
        }
```

```swift
        else {
            xml += "<\(startElement)>\(value)</\(startElement)>\n"
        }
    }
    return xml
}

func convertDictionaryToXML(dictionary: [String: Any],
startElement: String, isFirstElement: Bool) -> String {
    var xml = ""
    let arr = dictionary.keys
    if isFirstElement {
        xml += "<?xml version=\"1.0\" encoding=\"utf-8\"?>\n"
    }
    xml += "<\(startElement)>\n"
    for nodeName in arr {
        guard let nodeValue = dictionary[nodeName] else {
        continue }
        if let nodeValue = nodeValue as? [Any] {
            if !nodeValue.isEmpty {
                xml += convertArrayToXML(array: nodeValue,
                startElement: nodeName)
            }
        }
        else if let nodeValue = nodeValue as? [String: Any] {
            xml += convertDictionaryToXML(dictionary: nodeValue,
            startElement: nodeName, isFirstElement: false)
        }
        else {
            xml += "<\(nodeName)>\(nodeValue)</\(nodeName)>\n"
        }
    }
```

```
    xml += "</\(startElement)>\n"
    return xml.replacingOccurrences(of: "&", with: "&")
}
```

Usage

```
let dict: [String: Any] = ...
let xml = convertDictionaryToXML(dictionary: dict,
startElement: "root", isFirstElement: true)
```

Working with YAML

YAML (Yet Another Markup Language) is another popular format for storing and exchanging data. The advantage is that it's easy and human readable. The disadvantage is that YAML has indented delimiting (meaning that using leading spaces separates data levels), similarly to Python or GDScript. You can edit a YAML file in a simple text editor, but it's easy to make mistake.

One of the most popular usages of YAML is configuration files. Flutter apps use YAML for main configuration files, and Google Cloud also uses YAML for configuration of its services.

Luckily for us, there are many libraries on GitHub for parsing and/or generating YAML. One of them is Yams.

If you use CocoaPods, add this line to your Podfile:

```
pod 'Yams'
```

Then you can generate and parse YAML as shown in Recipe 2-5.

Recipe 2-5. Parsing and Generating YAML

```
import Yaml

// Generating YAML
let strYAML: String? = try? Yams.dump(object: dictionary)

// Parsing YAML
let loadedDictionary = try? Yams.load(yaml: mapYAML) as?
[String: Any]
```

URL-Encoded Strings

One more way to encode data is a URL-encoded string. It's useful for generating URLs with GET arguments, as well as POST data with `application/x-www-form-urlencoded` type.

A URL-encoded string is a text string consisting of key-value pairs separated by the ampersand symbol: `key1=value1&key2=value2&....` If you send it using the GET method (as a part of URL), it's separated from the main URL with a question mark: `https://some_website.com?key1=value1&key2=value2&....` As a POST data, it must be sent without any additional signs.

If you send data to a server, you probably have a set of keys to provide, and they must contain only Latin letters, numbers, and maybe underscores. A situation that includes values is more complicated – they can contain spaces, equal signs, or other *forbidden* characters. For this reason, we should encode them. Swift has a standard `String` method, `addingPercentEncoding(withAllowedCharacters:)`. Recipe 2-6 shows the full extension.

Recipe 2-6. URL-Encoding Argument Dictionary

```
public extension Dictionary where Key:
ExpressibleByStringLiteral {
    var urlEncodedString: String {
        var result: [String] = []
        for key in keys {
            let keyEncoded = "\(key)".addingPercentEncoding
            (withAllowedCharacters: .urlPathAllowed)!
            let valueEncoded = "\(self[key]!)".addingPercent
            Encoding(withAllowedCharacters: .urlPathAllowed)!
            result.append("\(keyEncoded)=\(valueEncoded)")
        }
        return result.joined(separator: "&")
    }
}
```

The usage is pretty straightforward:

```
let urlArgsDict: [String: Any] = [
    "firstName": "Luis Alberto",
    "lastName": "Lopez Garcia",
    "age": 15
]

let urlArgs = urlArgsDict.urlEncodedString
print(urlArgs)
```

The output will be as follows:

```
firstName=Luis%20Alberto&lastName=Lopez%20Garcia&age=15
```

It's totally suitable for sending to APIs:

```
https://my_api.com/register_user?firstName=Luis%20
Alberto&lastName=Lopez%20Garcia&age=15
```

Note   Registering users via GET requests is a bad practice. Still, this example demonstrates how you can encode any data for further sending it to the API.

Serialization and Deserialization

In previous sections, we discussed how to parse JSON into a `Dictionary` or an `Array`, how to extract typed data from them, and how to turn JSON from API into an instance of a custom class or struct. Here, we'll take a shortcut and turn JSON directly into an object.

Note   If you ever developed an app for Android, you know that to pass arguments to another Activity, you need to add them to an Intent. This is an example of serialization. You can also pass an object of custom class, but it must implement Parcelable interface. This interface has functions for serialization and deserialization of class data.

Serializing an Object

To make a data structure serializable, you need to implement an `Encodable` protocol. This protocol has one method – `encode(to: Encoder)`. You don't need to implement it yourself; it has a default implementation. But this default implementation works only if all the stored variables in your class or struct are `Encodable`. All basic types (`Int`,

String, Double, and others) are Encodable. All custom types are not, unless they implement Encodable. For example:

```
struct User: Encodable {
    var name: String
    var surname: String
    var age: Int
}
```

Why would we need it? Why make a struct or a class serializable (or Encodable as Swift calls it)? The magic starts when you need to turn it into JSON or save it to a file. The following example converts Encodable to Data and Dictionary:

```
struct User: Encodable {
    var name: String
    var surname: String
    var age: Int

    var asData: Data? {
        return try? JSONEncoder().encode(self)
    }

    var asDictionary: [String: Any]? {
        guard let data = self.asData else { return nil }
        return (try? JSONSerialization.jsonObject(with: data,
        options: .allowFragments)).flatMap { $0 as? [String: Any] }
    }
}
```

As you can see in the preceding listing, an Encodable object can be turned into a JSON-encoded Data or Swift Dictionary with just a couple of lines of code. You can add more variables to your Encodable structure, and they'll be automatically serialized by the Encodable protocol, or more precisely by the default implementation of its encode(to: Encodable) method.

```
let encUser = User(name: "John", surname: "Doe", age: 30)
let userDict = encUser.asDictionary
print(userDict ?? {})
```

Output

```
["surname": Doe, "name": John, "age": 30]
```

If for some reason serialization fails, nil will be returned.

As we discussed in the beginning, good code must be universal. It should be easy to copy it to another project without modifications or with minimum modifications. Swift extensions from Recipe 2-7 come to help.

Recipe 2-7. Encodable to JSON

```
public extension Encodable {
    var asJSONData: Data? {
        try? JSONEncoder().encode(self)
    }

    var asJSONString: String? {
        guard let data = self.asData else { return nil }
        return String(data: data, encoding: .utf8)
    }

    var asDictionary: [String: Any]? {
        guard let data = self.asData else { return nil }
        return (try? JSONSerialization.jsonObject(with:
        data, options: .allowFragments)).flatMap { $0 as?
        [String: Any] }
    }
}
```

Now everything conforming to the Encodable protocol will have methods asJSONData, asJSONDictionary, and asString. The following code snippet shows an encodable structure (which has methods asJSONData, asJSONString, and asDictionary):

```
struct User: Encodable {
    var name: String
    var surname: String
    var age: Int
}
```

These methods are extremely useful when you work with API accepting JSON-formatted arguments. Also, asData and asString methods can be used to save a file to flash memory, hard drive, or solid-state drive (if you write code compatible with macOS).

Deserializing an Object

Similarly to Encodable, Swift offers a Decodable protocol. Instead of a method, it declares a constructor init(from: Decoder). It has a default implementation as well.

Deserializing objects is a little more of a complicated task because of four reasons:

- The provided data structure may not have some fields declared in a Decodable structure.

- The provided data structure may have extra fields.

- The names in the provided data and the declared structures may not match.

- The types should be an exact match.

Before we continue, we'll need one more interface – Codable. It's not an independent interface; it's a composition of Encodable and Decodable, or in Swift terminology, it's a typealias.

```
typealias Codable = Decodable & Encodable
```

Generally, when we need to serialize a class, we need to deserialize it as well. Let's change our User structure to conform to Codable instead of Encodable.

```
struct User: Codable {
    var name: String
    var surname: String
    var age: Int
}
```

We don't write any extensions to Codable; it's just an alias. Instead, we extend a Decodable protocol as shown in Recipe 2-8.

Recipe 2-8. JSON to Decodable

```
public extension Decodable {
    init?(data: Data) {
        do {
            self = try JSONDecoder().decode(Self.self,
            from: data)
        } catch {
            return nil
        }
    }

    init?(dict: [String: Any]) {
        guard let jsonData = try? JSONSerialization.
        data(withJSONObject: dict, options: .fragmentsAllowed)
        else { return nil }
```

```
    do {
        self = try JSONDecoder().decode(Self.self, from:
        jsonData)
    } catch {
        return nil
    }
}

init?(jsonString: String) {
    guard let jsonData = jsonString.data(using: .utf8) else
    { return nil }
    do {
        self = try JSONDecoder().decode(Self.self, from:
        jsonData)
    } catch {
        return nil
    }
}
}
```

This code will return a valid object from a JSON-encoded String, Data, or Dictionary object, but only if the provided structure has name, surname, and age fields. And they must be spelled exactly like in the User declaration. The following is a user dictionary sample:

```
let decDict: [String: Any] = [
    "name": "John",
    "surname": "Doe",
    "age": 30
]

let decUser = User(dict: decDict)
```

What if one of the fields is missing? For example, we don't know the user's age. In this case, decUser will be nil. The problem can be fixed with making the fields optional. If some fields are required, they should be nonoptional; for example, the user ID is hardly optional. Other fields can be missing, and it's ok.

Another problem we've discussed previously is the type mismatch. Look at the following example:

```
struct User: Codable {
    var name: String
    var surname: String
    var age: Int?
}

let decDict: [String: Any] = [
    "name": "John",
    "surname": "Doe",
    "age": "30"
]

let decUser = User(dict: decDict)
```

The decUser object will have nil age. There are two solutions to this problem. The first solution is to take care of the server outputs. If you (or your team) write the API yourself, you can make strictly typed data. When you work with a third-party API, it's not an option. Here comes the second solution. You can manually define an init(from: Decoder) constructor. You need to do it for each class and struct individually – there's no universal solution here. You can see an example of this solution in Recipe 2-9.

Recipe 2-9. Manual Decoding

```swift
public struct User: Codable {
    var name: String
    var surname: String
    var age: Int?

    init(name: String, surname: String, age: Int?) {
        self.name = name
        self.surname = surname
        self.age = age
    }

    init(from decoder: Decoder) throws {
        let container = try decoder.container(keyedBy:
        CodingKeys.self)
        name = try container.decode(String.self, forKey: .name)
        surname = try container.decode(String.self, forKey:
        .surname)
        do {
            age = try container.decode(Int.self, forKey: .age)
        } catch DecodingError.typeMismatch {
            age = Int(try container.decode(String.self,
            forKey: .age))
        }
    }
}
```

Please note that if you add a custom constructor to a struct, you need to provide a default constructor if needed.

Even with this inconvenience, we still can define constructors in `Decodable` extension, which makes it more comfortable than using `Dictionary` extensions.

Coding Keys

JSON structures have key-value pairs, and it's not guaranteed that said keys will match the variable names in class or struct. There's a universal solution for both Encodable and Decodable – CodingKeys enumeration (Recipe 2-10):

Recipe 2-10. Using Coding Keys

```
enum CodingKeys: String, CodingKey {
    case name = "firstName"
    case surname = "lastName"

    case age
}
```

Example

```
struct User: Codable {
    var name: String
    var surname: String
    var age: Int?

    enum CodingKeys: String, CodingKey {
        case name = "firstName"
        case surname = "lastName"

        case age
    }
}

let decDict: [String: Any] = [
    "firstName": "John",
    "lastName": "Doe",
    "age": 30
]

let decUser = User(dict: decDict)
```

If fields have different names depending on the API, they can't be presented with serializable Swift types, and in other complex cases, using `Codable` may not be the best decision. Parsing data field by field from a `Dictionary` is more universal.

Using @propertyWrapper

What do we do if we need both the flexibility and the comfort of strict types? For example, when you need a flexible structure, but with constrained fields. The `Dictionary` class gives full flexibility, like JSON itself. Serialization requires strict structure declaration. There's another solution – `@propertyWrapper`.

It's an attribute that we give to a struct to declare it as a wrapper around its own property. In our case, property is data from a server presented as a `Dictionary`.

We'll make a wrapper around a structure representing the characteristics of an item in an electronics store. Different items may have different characteristics, and each of them has some limited range of values. It can be restriction of `String` length, minimum length, or any other characteristic. This approach helps to validate data and avoid showing values entered by mistake. Not all of them, unfortunately, but the most unrealistic.

This is not the only usage of `@propertyWrapper`, it can be used for all dynamic structures with some reasonable number of rules. At the same time, it's rarely a first-choice tool. Whenever possible, use parsing to native Swift structures.

We write two structures:

- `Item` – A struct holding all the data
- `ItemProjection` – A struct giving access to wrapped data with necessary constraints

An Item should be attributed as @propertyWrapper and have two fields:

- wrappedValue of type Dictionary

- projectedValue of type ItemProjection

To access fields, we address a wrappedValue by a variable name and a projectedValue by the same name but starting with a dollar sign. Recipe 2-11 shows the full example of using property wrappers.

Recipe 2-11. Using @propertyWrapper

```
public struct ItemProjection {
    var wrapper: Item

    public var title: String? {
        if let title = wrapper.wrappedValue.
        getString("title") {
            if title.count > ItemProjection.titleLengthLimit {
                let endIndex = title.index(title.startIndex,
                offsetBy: 100)
                return String(title[..<endIndex]) + "..."
            } else {
                return title
            }
        } else {
            return nil
        }
    }

    public var length: Double? {
        if let length = wrapper.wrappedValue.
        getDouble("length"),
            length > 0 {
            return length
```

```
        } else {
            return nil
        }
    }

    public var lengthInches: Double? {
        length?.cmAsInch
    }

    public var volts: Int {
        wrapper.wrappedValue.getInt("volts") ?? 220
    }

    public var watts: Int? {
        if let watts = wrapper.wrappedValue.getInt("watts"),
           watts > 0,
           watts < 10000 {
            return watts
        } else {
            return nil
        }
    }

    static let titleLengthLimit = 100
}

@propertyWrapper
public struct Item {
    public var wrappedValue: [String: Any]
    public var projectedValue: ItemProjection {
        ItemProjection(wrapper: self)
    }
```

```swift
    public init() {
        wrappedValue = [:]
    }

    public init(wrappedValue: [String: Any]) {
        self.wrappedValue = wrappedValue
    }
}
```

The preceding example gives fast access to title, length, volts, and watts. Before returning a value, it processes it. For example, if title is too long, it leaves only first 100 characters and adds three dots. Voltage is usually the same within the region, either 120 or 220 volts. If we know the location of the store, we don't need to add voltage to each item; we can skip it to use a default value.

Other values are checked on validity. If they're negative, zero, or too big, nil is returned instead not to show completely senseless data to a final user. As an option, an app can send a message to an analytics framework.

We also give access to length in inches (assuming that it's in centimeters in the database). This is done by extension cmAsInch shown later in this chapter.

Under the hood, it's still the same Dictionary, which means we can add any values we need. The structure is not fixed.

Note   This example uses extensions described in other chapters of this book.

As an example of usage, let's make a tiny electronics store, which sells only heaters (Company struct):

```
struct ElectronicsStore {
    @Item var heater = [
        "title": "Electric heater with too long title, that
        doesn't fit display or price tag. It should be
        shortened when requested.",
        "length": 50,
        "watts": 15000
    ]
}
```

We initialize them with dictionaries, which is what we usually get from APIs. Then we can easily access both the projected data and the Dictionary itself by accessing fields with @propertyWrapper:

```
var store = ElectronicsStore()
print(store.$heater.title ?? "No title")
print(store.$heater.length ?? "No length")
print(store.$heater.lengthInches ?? "No length in inches")
print(store.$heater.volts)
print(store.$heater.watts ?? "No watts")
```

This example produces the following output:

```
Electric heater with too long title, that doesn't fit display
or price tag. It should be shortened w...
50.0
19.68503937007874
220
No watts
```

Unit Conversion

In certain cases, you need to make a conversion within the same data type, for example, if you get a measurement in centimeters but you need the data in inches. Or you got miles from the API, but you understand distance in kilometers.

As conversion multipliers are not integers, it's better to use a `Double` type even if values don't have fractional parts.

Distance and Length Units

Let's assume that we need to calculate the total travel distance between London and Berlin. The airline company tells us that the flight is 580 miles long. The trip to the airport is 24300 yards. And to reach our hotel in Berlin, we need to travel 10400 meters. All is well, but you want the result in kilometers.

Computers were created for such calculations. After we write all the extensions, the resulting code will be like this:

```
let distanceInKm = (24300.0.yardsAsM + 580.0.milesAsM +
10400.0).mAsKm
```

Since iOS 10, which includes all available iOS versions now, you can use the `Measurement` struct. In all extensions related to conversions, we'll use it and show how it can be done under the hood in a comment. Using `Measurement` is a preferred method as it gives better precision and less potential mistakes. Use it unless you have exotic units not supported by iOS.

Another use case for direct conversions (see comments in the following code) is performance. If you need to make too many conversions, the `Measurement` class may be slower than multiplications and divisions.

In Recipe 2-12 we write extensions for the Double type. We have three commonly used imperial and three metric units:

- Inch

- Foot (ft)

- Mile

- Centimeter (cm)

- Meter (m)

- Kilometer (km)

Recipe 2-12. Distance/Length Conversion

```
public extension Double {
    var inchAsFt: Double {
        Measurement(value: self, unit: UnitLength.inches)
            .converted(to: UnitLength.feet)
            .value
        // self / 12.0
    }

    var inchAsMile: Double {
        Measurement(value: self, unit: UnitLength.inches)
            .converted(to: UnitLength.miles)
            .value
        // self / 63360.0
    }

    var inchAsCm: Double {
        Measurement(value: self, unit: UnitLength.inches)
            .converted(to: UnitLength.centimeters)
            .value
        // self * 2.54
    }
}
```

```swift
var inchAsM: Double {
    Measurement(value: self, unit: UnitLength.inches)
        .converted(to: UnitLength.meters)
        .value
    // self * 0.0254
}

var inchAsKm: Double {
    Measurement(value: self, unit: UnitLength.inches)
        .converted(to: UnitLength.kilometers)
        .value
    // self * 0.0000254
}

var ftAsInch: Double {
    Measurement(value: self, unit: UnitLength.feet)
        .converted(to: UnitLength.inches)
        .value
    // self * 12.0
}

var ftAsMile: Double {
    Measurement(value: self, unit: UnitLength.feet)
        .converted(to: UnitLength.miles)
        .value
    // self / 5280.0
}

var ftAsCm: Double {
    Measurement(value: self, unit: UnitLength.feet)
        .converted(to: UnitLength.centimeters)
        .value
    // self * 30.48
```

```
}

var ftAsM: Double {
    Measurement(value: self, unit: UnitLength.feet)
        .converted(to: UnitLength.meters)
        .value
    // self * 0.3048
}

var ftAsKm: Double {
    Measurement(value: self, unit: UnitLength.feet)
        .converted(to: UnitLength.kilometers)
        .value
    // self * 0.0003048
}

var mileAsInch: Double {
    Measurement(value: self, unit: UnitLength.miles)
        .converted(to: UnitLength.inches)
        .value
    // self * 63360.0
}

var mileAsFt: Double {
    Measurement(value: self, unit: UnitLength.miles)
        .converted(to: UnitLength.feet)
        .value
    // self * 5280.0
}

var mileAsCm: Double {
    Measurement(value: self, unit: UnitLength.miles)
        .converted(to: UnitLength.centimeters)
        .value
```

```
        // self * 160934.4
    }

    var mileAsM: Double {
        Measurement(value: self, unit: UnitLength.miles)
            .converted(to: UnitLength.meters)
            .value
        // self * 1609.344
    }

    var mileAsKm: Double {
        Measurement(value: self, unit: UnitLength.miles)
            .converted(to: UnitLength.kilometers)
            .value
        // self * 1.609344
    }

    var cmAsInch: Double {
        Measurement(value: self, unit: UnitLength.centimeters)
            .converted(to: UnitLength.inches)
            .value
        // self / 2.54
    }

    var cmAsFt: Double {
        Measurement(value: self, unit: UnitLength.centimeters)
            .converted(to: UnitLength.feet)
            .value
        // self / 30.48
    }

    var cmAsMile: Double {
        Measurement(value: self, unit: UnitLength.centimeters)
            .converted(to: UnitLength.miles)
```

```swift
        .value
    // self / 160934.4
}

var cmAsM: Double {
    Measurement(value: self, unit: UnitLength.centimeters)
        .converted(to: UnitLength.meters)
        .value
    // self * 0.01
}

var cmAsKm: Double {
    Measurement(value: self, unit: UnitLength.centimeters)
        .converted(to: UnitLength.kilometers)
        .value
    // self * 0.00001
}

var mAsInch: Double {
    Measurement(value: self, unit: UnitLength.meters)
        .converted(to: UnitLength.inches)
        .value
    // self * 39.3701
}

var mAsFt: Double {
    Measurement(value: self, unit: UnitLength.meters)
        .converted(to: UnitLength.feet)
        .value
    // self * 3.28084
}

var mAsMile: Double {
    Measurement(value: self, unit: UnitLength.meters)
```

```swift
        .converted(to: UnitLength.miles)
        .value
    // self / 1609.344
}

var mAsCm: Double {
    Measurement(value: self, unit: UnitLength.meters)
        .converted(to: UnitLength.centimeters)
        .value
    // self * 100.0
}

var mAsKm: Double {
    Measurement(value: self, unit: UnitLength.meters)
        .converted(to: UnitLength.kilometers)
        .value
    // self * 0.001
}

var kmAsInch: Double {
    Measurement(value: self, unit: UnitLength.kilometers)
        .converted(to: UnitLength.inches)
        .value
    // self * 39370.1
}

var kmAsFt: Double {
    Measurement(value: self, unit: UnitLength.kilometers)
        .converted(to: UnitLength.feet)
        .value
    // self * 3280.84
}

var kmAsMile: Double {
```

```swift
    Measurement(value: self, unit: UnitLength.kilometers)
        .converted(to: UnitLength.miles)
        .value
    // self / 1.609344
}

var kmAsCm: Double {
    Measurement(value: self, unit: UnitLength.kilometers)
        .converted(to: UnitLength.centimeters)
        .value
    // self * 100000.0
}

var kmAsM: Double {
    Measurement(value: self, unit: UnitLength.kilometers)
        .converted(to: UnitLength.meters)
        .value
    // self * 1000.0
}
}
```

Length and distance units are not the only difference between the metric and the imperial system. There are area, volume, and weight units as well. Let's write extensions for them all.

Area Units

Commonly used area units are

- Square foot (sq. ft. or sqft in the code below)
- Rood
- Acre

- Square meter (sq. m. or sqm in the code below)

- Square centimeter (sq. cm. or sqcm in the code below)

- Hectare (ha. or hect in the code below)

As rood is not in the UnitArea class, we'll make conversion through acres, assuming that 4 roods equal to 1 acre. Recipe 2-13 shows the full extension.

Recipe 2-13. Area Conversion

```
public extension Double {
    var sqftAsRood: Double {
        Measurement(value: self, unit: UnitArea.squareFeet)
            .converted(to: UnitArea.acres)
            .value
            .acreAsRood
        // self / 10890.0
    }

    var sqftAsAcre: Double {
        Measurement(value: self, unit: UnitArea.squareFeet)
            .converted(to: UnitArea.acres)
            .value
        // self / 43560.0
    }

    var sqftAsSqm: Double {
        Measurement(value: self, unit: UnitArea.squareFeet)
            .converted(to: UnitArea.squareMeters)
            .value
        // self / 10.7639
    }

    var sqftAsSqcm: Double {
        Measurement(value: self, unit: UnitArea.squareFeet)
```

```swift
        .converted(to: UnitArea.squareCentimeters)
        .value
    // self * 929.03
}

var sqftAsHect: Double {
    Measurement(value: self, unit: UnitArea.squareFeet)
        .converted(to: UnitArea.hectares)
        .value
    // self / 107639.1
}

var roodAsSqft: Double {
    Measurement(value: self.roodAsAcre, unit:
    UnitArea.acres)
        .converted(to: UnitArea.squareFeet)
        .value
    // self * 10890.0
}

var roodAsAcre: Double {
    self / 4.0
}

var roodAsSqm: Double {
    Measurement(value: self.roodAsAcre, unit:
    UnitArea.acres)
        .converted(to: UnitArea.squareMeters)
        .value
    // self * 1011.7141056
}

var roodAsSqcm: Double {
```

```
    Measurement(value: self.roodAsAcre, unit:
    UnitArea.acres)
        .converted(to: UnitArea.squareCentimeters)
        .value
    // self * 10117141.056
}

var roodAsHect: Double {
    Measurement(value: self.roodAsAcre, unit:
    UnitArea.acres)
        .converted(to: UnitArea.hectares)
        .value
    // self * 0.10021786
}

var acreAsSqft: Double {
    Measurement(value: self, unit: UnitArea.acres)
        .converted(to: UnitArea.squareFeet)
        .value
    // self * 43560.0
}

var acreAsRood: Double {
    self * 4.0
}

var acreAsSqm: Double {
    Measurement(value: self, unit: UnitArea.acres)
        .converted(to: UnitArea.squareMeters)
        .value
    // self * 4046.8564224
}
```

```
var acreAsSqcm: Double {
    Measurement(value: self, unit: UnitArea.acres)
        .converted(to: UnitArea.squareCentimeters)
        .value
    // self * 40468564.224
}

var acreAsHect: Double {
    Measurement(value: self, unit: UnitArea.acres)
        .converted(to: UnitArea.hectares)
        .value
    // self / 2.47105
}

var sqmAsSqft: Double {
    Measurement(value: self, unit: UnitArea.squareMeters)
        .converted(to: UnitArea.squareFeet)
        .value
    // self * 10.7639
}

var sqmAsRood: Double {
    Measurement(value: self, unit: UnitArea.squareMeters)
        .converted(to: UnitArea.acres)
        .value
        .acreAsRood
    // self / 1011.7141056
}

var sqmAsAcre: Double {
    Measurement(value: self, unit: UnitArea.squareMeters)
        .converted(to: UnitArea.acres)          .
        .value
```

```swift
        // self / 4046.8564224
    }

    var sqmAsSqcm: Double {
        Measurement(value: self, unit: UnitArea.squareMeters)
            .converted(to: UnitArea.squareCentimeters)
            .value
        // self * 10000.0
    }

    var sqmAsHect: Double {
        Measurement(value: self, unit: UnitArea.squareMeters)
            .converted(to: UnitArea.hectares)
            .value
        // self * 0.0001
    }

    var sqcmAsSqft: Double {
        Measurement(value: self, unit: UnitArea.
        squareCentimeters)
            .converted(to: UnitArea.squareFeet)
            .value
        // self / 929.03
    }

    var sqcmAsRood: Double {
        Measurement(value: self, unit: UnitArea.
        squareCentimeters)
            .converted(to: UnitArea.acres)
            .value
            .acreAsRood
        // self / 10117141.056
    }
```

```
var sqcmAsAcre: Double {
    Measurement(value: self, unit: UnitArea.
    squareCentimeters)
        .converted(to: UnitArea.acres)
        .value
    // self / 40468564.224
}

var sqcmAsSqm: Double {
    Measurement(value: self, unit: UnitArea.
    squareCentimeters)
        .converted(to: UnitArea.squareMeters)
        .value
    // self * 0.0001
}

var sqcmAsHect: Double {
    Measurement(value: self, unit: UnitArea.
    squareCentimeters)
        .converted(to: UnitArea.hectares)
        .value
    // self * 0.00000001
}

var hectAsSqft: Double {
    Measurement(value: self, unit: UnitArea.
    squareCentimeters)
        .converted(to: UnitArea.squareFeet)
        .value
    // self * 107639.1
}

var hectAsRood: Double {
```

```
        Measurement(value: self, unit: UnitArea.hectares)
            .converted(to: UnitArea.acres)
            .value
            .acreAsRood
        // self * 9.97826087
    }

    var hectAsAcre: Double {
        Measurement(value: self, unit: UnitArea.hectares)
            .converted(to: UnitArea.acres)
            .value
        // self * 2.47105
    }

    var hectAsSqm: Double {
        Measurement(value: self, unit: UnitArea.hectares)
            .converted(to: UnitArea.squareMeters)
            .value
        // self * 10000
    }

    var hectAsSqcm: Double {
        Measurement(value: self, unit: UnitArea.hectares)
            .converted(to: UnitArea.squareCentimeters)
            .value
        // self * 100000000
    }
}
```

Volume Units

Recipe 2-14 shows extensions converting volume units. Commonly used volume units are

- Fluid ounce (fl. oz)

- Pint

- Gallon

- Milliliter (ml)

- Liter (l)

Recipe 2-14. Volume Conversion

```
public extension Double {
    var flozAsPint: Double {
        Measurement(value: self, unit: UnitVolume.fluidOunces)
            .converted(to: UnitVolume.pints)
            .value
        // self / 16.0
    }

    var flozAsGallon: Double {
        Measurement(value: self, unit: UnitVolume.fluidOunces)
            .converted(to: UnitVolume.gallons)
            .value
        // self / 128.0
    }

    var flozAsMl: Double {
        Measurement(value: self, unit: UnitVolume.fluidOunces)
            .converted(to: UnitVolume.milliliters)
            .value
        // self * 29.5735
    }
```

```swift
var flozAsL: Double {
    Measurement(value: self, unit: UnitVolume.fluidOunces)
        .converted(to: UnitVolume.liters)
        .value
    // self * 0.0295735
}

var pintAsFloz: Double {
    Measurement(value: self, unit: UnitVolume.pints)
        .converted(to: UnitVolume.fluidOunces)
        .value
    // self * 16.0
}

var pintAsGallon: Double {
    Measurement(value: self, unit: UnitVolume.pints)
        .converted(to: UnitVolume.gallons)
        .value
    // self / 8.0
}

var pintAsMl: Double {
    Measurement(value: self, unit: UnitVolume.pints)
        .converted(to: UnitVolume.milliliters)
        .value
    // self * 473.176
}

var pintAsL: Double {
    Measurement(value: self, unit: UnitVolume.pints)
        .converted(to: UnitVolume.liters)
        .value
    // self * 0.473176
}
```

```swift
var gallonAsFloz: Double {
    Measurement(value: self, unit: UnitVolume.gallons)
        .converted(to: UnitVolume.fluidOunces)
        .value
    // self * 128.0
}

var gallonAsPint: Double {
    Measurement(value: self, unit: UnitVolume.gallons)
        .converted(to: UnitVolume.pints)
        .value
    // self * 8.0
}

var gallonAsMl: Double {
    Measurement(value: self, unit: UnitVolume.gallons)
        .converted(to: UnitVolume.milliliters)
        .value
    // self * 3785.41
}

var gallonAsL: Double {
    Measurement(value: self, unit: UnitVolume.gallons)
        .converted(to: UnitVolume.liters)
        .value
    // self * 3.78541
}

var mlAsFloz: Double {
    Measurement(value: self, unit: UnitVolume.milliliters)
        .converted(to: UnitVolume.fluidOunces)
        .value
    // self / 29.5735
}
```

```swift
var mlAsPint: Double {
    Measurement(value: self, unit: UnitVolume.milliliters)
        .converted(to: UnitVolume.pints)
        .value
    // self / 473.176
}

var mlAsGallon: Double {
    Measurement(value: self, unit: UnitVolume.milliliters)
        .converted(to: UnitVolume.gallons)
        .value
    // self / 3785.41
}

var mlAsL: Double {
    Measurement(value: self, unit: UnitVolume.milliliters)
        .converted(to: UnitVolume.liters)
        .value
    // self * 0.001
}

var lAsFloz: Double {
    Measurement(value: self, unit: UnitVolume.liters)
        .converted(to: UnitVolume.fluidOunces)
        .value
    // self / 0.0295735
}

var lAsPint: Double {
    Measurement(value: self, unit: UnitVolume.liters)
        .converted(to: UnitVolume.pints)
        .value
    // self / 0.473176
}
```

```
var lAsGallon: Double {
    Measurement(value: self, unit: UnitVolume.liters)
        .converted(to: UnitVolume.gallons)
        .value
    // self / 3.78541
}

var lAsMl: Double {
    Measurement(value: self, unit: UnitVolume.liters)
        .converted(to: UnitVolume.milliliters)
        .value
    // self * 1000.0
}
}
```

Weight Units

In Recipe 2-15 you can find weight conversions. Commonly used weight units are

- Ounce (oz)
- Pound (lbs)
- Stone (st)
- Gram (g)
- Kilogram (kg)

Recipe 2-15. Weight Conversion

```
public extension Double {
    var ozAsLbs: Double {
        Measurement(value: self, unit: UnitMass.ounces)
```

```
            .converted(to: UnitMass.pounds)
            .value
        // self / 16.0
    }

    var ozAsSt: Double {
        Measurement(value: self, unit: UnitMass.ounces)
            .converted(to: UnitMass.stones)
            .value
        // self / 224.0
    }

    var ozAsG: Double {
        Measurement(value: self, unit: UnitMass.ounces)
            .converted(to: UnitMass.grams)
            .value
        // self * 28.3495
    }

    var ozAsKg: Double {
        Measurement(value: self, unit: UnitMass.ounces)
            .converted(to: UnitMass.kilograms)
            .value
        // self * 0.0283495
    }

    var lbsAsOz: Double {
        Measurement(value: self, unit: UnitMass.pounds)
            .converted(to: UnitMass.ounces)
            .value
        // self * 16.0
    }
```

```swift
var lbsAsSt: Double {
    Measurement(value: self, unit: UnitMass.pounds)
        .converted(to: UnitMass.stones)
        .value
    // self / 14.0
}

var lbsAsG: Double {
    Measurement(value: self, unit: UnitMass.pounds)
        .converted(to: UnitMass.grams)
        .value
    // self * 453.592
}

var lbsAsKg: Double {
    Measurement(value: self, unit: UnitMass.pounds)
        .converted(to: UnitMass.kilograms)
        .value
    // self * 0.453592
}

var stAsOz: Double {
    Measurement(value: self, unit: UnitMass.stones)
        .converted(to: UnitMass.ounces)
        .value
    // self * 224.0
}

var stAsLbs: Double {
    Measurement(value: self, unit: UnitMass.stones)
        .converted(to: UnitMass.pounds)
        .value
    // self * 14.0
}
```

```swift
var stAsG: Double {
    Measurement(value: self, unit: UnitMass.stones)
        .converted(to: UnitMass.grams)
        .value
    // self * 6350.29
}

var stAsKg: Double {
    Measurement(value: self, unit: UnitMass.stones)
        .converted(to: UnitMass.kilograms)
        .value
    // self * 6.35029
}

var gAsOz: Double {
    Measurement(value: self, unit: UnitMass.grams)
        .converted(to: UnitMass.ounces)
        .value
    // self / 28.3495
}

var gAsLbs: Double {
    Measurement(value: self, unit: UnitMass.grams)
        .converted(to: UnitMass.pounds)
        .value
    // self / 453.592
}

var gAsSt: Double {
    Measurement(value: self, unit: UnitMass.grams)
        .converted(to: UnitMass.stones)
        .value
    // self / 6350.29
}
```

```swift
    var gAsKg: Double {
        Measurement(value: self, unit: UnitMass.grams)
            .converted(to: UnitMass.kilograms)
            .value
        // self * 0.001
    }

    var kgAsOz: Double {
        Measurement(value: self, unit: UnitMass.kilograms)
            .converted(to: UnitMass.ounces)
            .value
        // self / 0.0283495
    }

    var kgAsLbs: Double {
        Measurement(value: self, unit: UnitMass.kilograms)
            .converted(to: UnitMass.pounds)
            .value
        // self / 0.453592
    }

    var kgAsSt: Double {
        Measurement(value: self, unit: UnitMass.kilograms)
            .converted(to: UnitMass.stones)
            .value
        // self / 6.35029
    }

    var kgAsG: Double {
        Measurement(value: self, unit: UnitMass.kilograms)
            .converted(to: UnitMass.grams)
            .value
        // self * 1000.0
    }
}
```

Summary

We had a look at three popular data representations: JSON, XML, and YAML. JSON is the most popular for data exchange, but other formats also have their place in the IT world. We also reviewed `Encodable` and `Decodable` structures, the core of data serialization in Swift. Property wrappers may be useful as well if you want to keep flexibility, add data processing, but keep data structured.

Finally, we added semantics to data and introduced number units and conversion between them.

In the next chapter, we'll switch to one of the most popular data types in all modern languages – `String`. We already saw that it can represent literally everything using JSON. But it can also be analyzed, verified, used to represent binary data, secure data, and much more.

CHAPTER 3

Working with Strings

Strings are also data – they're arrays of bytes. But unlike simple `Data`, the `String` class knows how to interpret that data. To interpret data correctly, we need to know encoding. The most widespread options are UTF-8 and UTF-16, also known as Unicode.

UTF-8 uses one to four bytes to encode one character. Latin characters from the ASCII range use one byte. If the text contains only Latin characters, spaces, and standard punctuation symbols, ASCII and UTF-8 text strings are identical.

UTF-16 uses two of four bytes per character. As two bytes make 65536 combinations, they cover most of existing symbols. But not all of them. That's why some symbols need four bytes.

We don't need to know which encoding is used inside `String` or `Character` structures (yes, in Swift, they're defined as structs, not classes). But knowing that it's a `String`, we can get a lot of information about stored data compared to a `Data` object.

We know that text strings consist of characters, so we can get one of them. We can also get a range, which is called a `Substring`. And we don't need to think how wide is one `Character`; Swift will calculate width in bytes automatically. We can remove whitespaces and/or newlines, we can make it lowercase or uppercase, and we can analyze its content and much more.

© Alexander Nekrasov 2022
A. Nekrasov, *Swift Recipes for iOS Developers*,
https://doi.org/10.1007/978-1-4842-8098-0_3

Analyzing String Content

Let's suppose for a minute that we have a `String` object. We want to know what's inside. Does it have Latin letters? Or numbers? Is it a strong password? A valid email?

UIKit offers two classes to get text input from the user: `UITextField` and `UITextView`. Both of them return data as a test. Even if we request a number from the user (their age, bank card number, a number they should guess) and choose an on-screen keyboard with numbers only, we'll get a `String` (Recipe 3-1).

Recipe 3-1. Checking String for Digits and Letters

```
public extension StringProtocol {
    var containsOnlyDigits: Bool {
        let notDigits = NSCharacterSet.decimalDigits.inverted
        return rangeOfCharacter(from: notDigits, options:
        String.CompareOptions.literal, range: nil) == nil
    }

    var containsOnlyLetters: Bool {
        let notLetters = NSCharacterSet.letters.inverted
        return rangeOfCharacter(from: notLetters, options:
        String.CompareOptions.literal, range: nil) == nil
    }

    var containsIllegalCharacters: Bool {
        rangeOfCharacter(from: NSCharacterSet.
        illegalCharacters, options: String.CompareOptions.
        literal, range: nil) != nil
    }

    var containsOnlyPasswordAllowed: Bool {
        var allowedCharacters = CharacterSet()
```

```swift
    allowedCharacters.insert(charactersIn: "!"..."~")
    let forbiddenCharacters = allowedCharacters.inverted
    return rangeOfCharacter(from: forbiddenCharacters,
    options: String.CompareOptions.literal, range:
    nil) == nil
}

var isAlphanumeric: Bool {
    let notAlphanumeric = NSCharacterSet.decimalDigits.
    union(NSCharacterSet.letters).inverted
    return rangeOfCharacter(from: notAlphanumeric, options:
    String.CompareOptions.literal, range: nil) == nil
}

var containsLetters: Bool {
    rangeOfCharacter(from: NSCharacterSet.letters, options:
    String.CompareOptions.literal, range: nil) != nil
}

var containsDigits: Bool {
    rangeOfCharacter(from: NSCharacterSet.decimalDigits,
    options: String.CompareOptions.literal, range:
    nil) != nil
}

var containsUppercaseLetters: Bool {
    rangeOfCharacter(from: NSCharacterSet.uppercaseLetters,
    options: String.CompareOptions.literal, range:
    nil) != nil
}

var containsLowercaseLetters: Bool {
```

```
        rangeOfCharacter(from: NSCharacterSet.lowercaseLetters,
        options: String.CompareOptions.literal, range:
        nil) != nil
    }

    var containsNonAlphanumericCharacters: Bool {
        let notAlphanumeric = NSCharacterSet.decimalDigits.
        union(NSCharacterSet.letters).inverted
        return rangeOfCharacter(from: notAlphanumeric, options:
        String.CompareOptions.literal, range: nil) != nil
    }
}
```

These three extensions allow us to make fast (but simple) content analysis:

- containsOnlyDigits returns true if String contains nothing but digits. No decimal separators, no spaces, no special characters. We can get similar results by casting String to Int, but without the potential overflow problem, and we handle negative numbers differently.

- containsOnlyLetters returns true if String contains nothing but letters. Without modifications, it doesn't have much use, but we'll update it later to make it more powerful.

- isAlphanumeric returns true if String contains letters and numbers. For example, a Firestore document ID is always alphanumeric, as well as the String representation of MD5 hashes.

As we're discussing real-life examples, let's talk about use cases. Registration forms may contain

- First and last names
- Email address
- Password
- Phone number
- Gender
- Date of birth or age
- Credit card information
- Address

When Apple reviewers see such a list on the registration screen, they reject the app. But any of these fields may be necessary for specific functionality.

We'll leave address verification behind the scope, as it's specific for every country, and discuss other fields. For all extensions described in the following, we'll use names starting with isValid, for example, `isValidName` and `isValidEmail`, and write them as calculated properties.

Note   Using function or calculated property is always the programmer's choice. There's a popular opinion that calculated properties should be used when the function reflects a property of an object and doesn't change it.

First, Last, and Other Names

Depending on your app's region and your preferences, it can be one field for the full name, separate fields for the first and last names, or a more detailed set of fields, including middle name or patronymic. They can only contain letters, spaces, dashes, and maybe the dot symbol for titles like "Jr." or "Mr.". An example of name verification is shown in Recipe 3-2.

Recipe 3-2. Name Verification

```
public extension StringProtocol {
    var isValidName: Bool {
        let allowedCharactgers = NSCharacterSet.letters.
        union(NSCharacterSet.whitespaces).union(CharacterSet
        (charactersIn: ".-"))
        let forbiddenCharacters = allowedCharactgers.inverted
        return rangeOfCharacter(from: forbiddenCharacters,
        options: String.CompareOptions.literal, range:
        nil) == nil
    }
}
```

This extension merges three character sets:

- Whitespaces

- Letters

- Characters . and -

It inverts the resulting set and verifies that no forbidden characters are found in the String.

Note   In May 2020, famous business magnate Elon Musk (PayPal, Tesla, SpaceX) and Canadian musician Grimes had a son who immediately got his share of fame because of a very unusual name – X Æ A-12. However, the Office of Vital Records in California requires that names contain only the 26 alphabetical characters of the English language (plus hyphens and apostrophes); thus, this name was rejected. The couple had to change the name to X AE A-XII, where X is the first name and AE A-XII is the middle name. Just like the administration of California, our extension would reject the first option and accept the final one.

Email Address

This topic always causes a lot of controversy. While some developers try to restrict email addresses to a problem-free territory, others want to give users as much freedom as possible – up to lack of verification on the client's side. For example, is the email address *root@localhost* valid? It actually is. But when the user registers in an app, there's not much use to it, as we can't send any emails to it and it's not unique.

We'll discuss email verification in the context of user registration. And we will allow only emails with the following format: some-string@some-domain.ext, where *some-string* may contain Latin letters, numbers, and the symbols ., _, -, %, and +; *some-domain* may contain Latin letters, numbers, -, and . for subdomains; and *ext* must have only Latin letters and be no shorter than two characters and no longer than 64.

Analysis can be done with regular expressions as shown in Recipe 3-3. We won't discuss regular expressions in detail. In short, it's a pattern. There's standard syntax for regular expressions, which is universal for different platforms and languages. Regular expression for email verification looks like this: [A-Z0-9a-z._%+-]+@[A-Za-z0-9.-]+\\.[A-Za-z]{2,64}.

It's not the only option when it comes to regular expressions. There are other options, but this expression works quite well and has been tested by hundreds of thousands of users. It can be used with a Firebase Auth framework, filtering unnecessary requests, but it's even more useful if you have a custom back end.

Recipe 3-3. Email Verification

```
extension StringProtocol {
    var isValidEmail: Bool {
        let emailRegEx = "[A-Z0-9a-z._%+-]+@[A-Za-z0-9.-]+\\.
        [A-Za-z]{2,64}"
```

```
        let emailTest = NSPredicate(format: "SELF MATCHES %@",
        emailRegEx)
        return emailTest.evaluate(with: self)
    }
}
```

Password

How annoying it is when you try to set "12345678" as your password and the app or website you're trying to set the password for won't allow, isn't it? Depending on the specifics of your app, the minimum allowed strength of a password should be different. If you're writing an app for a financial service, the password should be strong. If it's a personal calorie counter or an online video streaming service, you may be allowed to use a much more simple password. But in any case, there are passwords that should never be allowed, for example, "12345678".

The basic recommendations for passwords are as follows:

- They should contain at least one capital and one lowercase letter.

- They should contain at least one digit.

- They should contain at least one special character (punctuation mark, percent sign, dollar sign, or similar).

- They shouldn't have spaces, new lines, or tabs.

The last recommendation is a standard for most services, though it's not a strict rule. The previous recommendations are not so strict either, but it's a good practice to force the user to fulfil at least two of three.

The extension from Recipe 3-4 will verify that

- The string has only alphanumeric characters, plus some special characters (dot, comma, and others)

- The string has at least one English letter

- Two of these three conditions are met:

    - The string has both lowercase and capital letters.

    - The string has at least one numeric character.

    - The string has at least one allowed nonalphanumeric character.

Recipe 3-4. Password Validation

```
public extension StringProtocol {
    var isValidPassword: Bool {
        if containsIllegalCharacters ||
        !containsOnlyPasswordAllowed {
            return false
        }
        if !containsLetters {
            return false
        }
        var strength = 0
        if containsUppercaseLetters {
            strength += 1
        }
        if containsLowercaseLetters {
            strength += 1
        }
```

```
        if containsDigits {
            strength += 1
        }
        if containsNonAlphanumericCharacters {
            strength += 1
        }
        return strength >= 3
    }
}
```

Phone Number

Phone number verification is another popular operation. Undoubtedly, the server should make its own verification. But to avoid unnecessary traffic, provide fast error handling, and protect the server from potentially harmful requests, it's better to make the verification on the client's side as well.

While email address has more flexibility, phone numbers are limited with digits, plus sign and separators. The length range is narrow, and it varies from country to country. We can make basic verifications with regular expressions, but there is a more efficient way that we will discuss in the following.

The PhoneNumberKit library allows to parse phone numbers, verify their validity, and convert local phone numbers to an international format. In Recipe 3-5 we use this library to verify phone number validity. Let's add it to our Podfile:

```
pod 'PhoneNumberKit'
```

Recipe 3-5. Phone Number Verification

```
import PhoneNumberKit

public extension String {
```

```
var isValidPhoneNumber: Bool {
    do {
        try phoneNumberKit.parse("+33 6 89 017383")
        return true
    }
    catch {
        return false
    }
}
}
```

Gender

Gender selection shouldn't be in the registration form unless it's absolutely necessary. And if it is, try to make it optional. First, Apple requires your app to follow their *Guidelines*, which don't allow asking for unnecessary personal data. Convincing Apple that knowing the user's gender is necessary for the app functionality will be complicated. Second, it's unclear which list of genders to present to the user. If you present a choice between male and female only, you can upset the LGBTQ+ community. They are potential clients as well, so that's something to keep in mind.

If you still decided to add gender selection in your app, add it as a selection of two or more options without using the keyboard. This will make string analysis unnecessary.

Date of Birth

This field may be necessary if you have adult content. Age (or date of birth) selection can give you an idea of which content to show or hide. If your app sells food and drinks, you can hide alcohol and tobacco from minors (specific age restriction depends on the region).

The best practice is to add a date selector component to your UI, for example, UIDatePicker. Then you format the date using one of the date formatters matching your region. For example:

```
let selectedDate = Date()
let dateFormatter = DateFormatter()
dateFormatter.dateFormat = "MM/dd/yyyy"
dateFormatter.string(from: selectedDate)
```

Date formats vary from country to country. Your app should use the format that is commonly used in your region or offer several options depending on device settings.

If you need to work with user input and you don't have an option to add a date picker, NSDataDetector comes to help (see Recipe 3-6).

Recipe 3-6. Parsing Date from String

```
public extension String {
    var asDate: Date? {
        let range = NSRange(location: 0, length: count)
        return try? NSDataDetector(types: NSTextCheckingResult.
        CheckingType.date.rawValue)
                .matches(in: self, range: range)
            .compactMap(\.date)
            .first
    }
}
```

This extension will try to convert any user-typed string to a Date object, or return nil if it's not possible.

Credit Card Information

If you want to add any paid functionalities to the app, you need to use In-App Purchases. Apple won't allow you to use direct payment; otherwise, the app will be rejected.

On the other hand, if you sell goods or services that are not part of the app, you may need to get the user's credit card number. Typical examples are food delivery apps, online shops, and booking services.

The most popular credit cards have these four components:

- Number

- Expiration month and year

- Security code (CVC/CVV)

- Name

Depending on the card type, the number varies from 16 to 19 digits. Usually, the number is separated by spaces after each four digits, but it's not compulsory. For that reason, we will remove all spaces before verification.

When it comes to expiration month and year, everything is pretty straightforward. Month is a number from 1 to 12, and year has two or four digits. We'll verify if the expiration date is during the current month of the current year or later.

The security code is always a number. It has three or four digits. As it can start with leading zeros, integer representation is a number between 0 and 9999.

The verification of names is identical to the verification of the user name on the registration form, so we'll simply reuse our existing code. Full credit card verification code is shown in Recipe 3-7.

Recipe 3-7. Credit Card Validation

```
public struct CreditCard {
    public var number: String
    public var expMonth: Int
    public var expYear: Int
    public var securityCode: Int
    public var nameOnCard: String

    public init(number: String, expMonth: Int, expYear: Int,
    securityCode: Int, nameOnCard: String) {
        self.number = number
        self.expMonth = expMonth
        self.expYear = expYear
        self.securityCode = securityCode
        self.nameOnCard = nameOnCard
    }

    var isNumberValid: Bool {
        let numberProcessed = String(number.filter { !"
        ".contains($0) })
        return numberProcessed.containsOnlyDigits &&
        numberProcessed.count >= 16 && numberProcessed.count <= 19
    }

    var isExpirationValid: Bool {
        if expMonth < 1 || expMonth > 12 {
            return false
        }

        let expYear4Digits = (expYear < 100) ? expYear + 2000
        : expYear

        let calendar = Calendar(identifier: .gregorian)
```

```
    let monthToday = calendar.component(.month,
    from: Date())
    let yearToday = calendar.component(.year, from: Date())

    switch expYear4Digits {
    case ..<yearToday: return false
    case yearToday: return expMonth >= monthToday
    default: return true
    }
}

var isSecurityCodeValid: Bool {
    securityCode < 10000
}

var isNameValid: Bool {
    nameOnCard.isValidName
}

public var isCardValid: Bool {
    isNumberValid && isExpirationValid &&
    isSecurityCodeValid && isNameValid
}
}
```

Unlike most of our previous recipes, this one is a class, not an extension. A credit card number is a whole thing – for example, we validate the month and year together, so we won't separate them into a group of extensions.

Before that, the validation structure needs to be filled with data. Use the isCardValid property to get the result as a Boolean value. If you need to know which component of a number is invalid, use isNameValid, isNumberValid, and other functions.

Note   In this chapter, we discuss work with information, not UI, but sometimes, it may be useful to try code in an app, not in a playground. For this, you can use libraries for entering (scanning) and visualizing bank cards. In Figure 3-1, you can see visualization made by the CreditCardView library (`https://github.com/jboullianne/CreditCardView`). For scanning, you can use card. io (`https://github.com/card-io/card.io-iOS-SDK`).

Figure 3-1. *Credit card visualization in an iOS app*

Base64 and Hex Encoding

Oftentimes, we need to present Data in the form of a String. We may need it for debug output, for passing it to the server, or for JSON integration. There are two common ways to do it: Base64 and hex encoding.

Base64 Encoding

Base64 is a way to represent binary data as a text string. It splits data into 6-bit fragments and encodes it using human-readable characters:

- 26 uppercase Latin letters

- 26 lowercase Latin letters

- 10 digits

- + (plus sign)

- / (slash sign)

As we can only encode integer amount of bytes, and 1 byte equals 8 bits, the data length needs to be divisible by three. If it isn't, padding is used. The equal sign (=) is used for padding when you need to add empty bits to the end of data. By adding one or two paddings, you can always get a number of bits, which is divisible by both 6 and 8.

The advantage of Base64 encoding is that characters used for encoding are basic ASCII characters, which means they're represented the same in all 1-byte encodings.

Table 3-1 encodes the word `"Swift"` into Base64.

Table 3-1. *Binary representation of the word "Swift"*

S	w	i	f	t
0101 0011	0111 0111	0110 1001	0110 0110	0111 0100

Totally, we get 40 bytes, which is not divisible by 6, so we'll need padding. Table 3-2 splits it into 6-bit fragments.

Table 3-2. *Base64 representation of the word "Swift"*

010100	110111	011101	101001	011001	100111	0100XX
U	3	d	p	Z	n	Q=

Result: "Swift" -> U3dpZnQ=.

Encoding ASCII text to Base64 doesn't usually make sense, but using the same method, we can encode pictures, audio files, and basically anything to strings. It's more compact than hex encoding, using two symbols to encode each byte, and it's easily encodable and decodable. Typical examples of Base64-encoded binaries are email attachments. Recipe 3-8 shows how to decode from Base64 and encode to this format.

Recipe 3-8. Encoding and Decoding Base64

```
let base64String = "U3dpZnQ="
let data = Data(base64Encoded: base64String)!

// Check if we got correct text
let decodedString = String(data: data, encoding: .utf8)!
print(decodedString)

let base64Again = data.base64EncodedString()
print(base64Again)
```

In the preceding example, we decode Base64 String into Data using the optional constructor Data(base64Encoded:). In this case, we use force unwrapping because we know that it's valid. Keep in mind that in production code, it's not an advisable practice.

Data has a method base64EncodedString for encoding. These are standard Swift functions; no extra code is needed in this case.

Hex Encoding

Hex representation is more human-readable and more simple. We don't need any paddings; each byte is represented with two hex symbols. A hex symbol is a number from 0 to 9 or a letter from A to F. Each hex symbol encodes 4 bytes of information.

Let's repeat the "Swift" encoding string (Table 3-3).

Table 3-3. *Binary representation of the word "Swift"*

S	w	i	f	t
0101 0011	0111 0111	0110 1001	0110 0110	0111 0100

Table 3-4 shows how it looks in hex representation.

Table 3-4. *Hex representation of the word "Swift"*

0101	0011	0111	0111	0110	1001	0110	0110	0111	0100
5	3	7	7	6	9	6	6	7	4

As you can see, hex is longer than Base64. And in this particular case, it looks like a number. But with some practice, you can learn to read it. For example, S will always be encoded to 53, w to 77, and so on.

Note   In source code, hex numbers start with 0x to avoid confusion with decimal numbers. If hex is represented as a String, it's wrapped in quotes but doesn't have any prefixes.

Let's switch to code. The extension from Recipe 3-9 offers a computed property turning Data to hex-encoded String and optional constructor doing the opposite.

Recipe 3-9. Converting Hex String to Data and Back

```swift
public extension Data {
    init?(hexString: String) {
        if hexString.count % 2 != 0 {
            return nil
        }

        let allowedCharacters = CharacterSet(charactersIn:
        "01234567890abcdefABCDEF")
        if hexString.rangeOfCharacter(from: allowedCharacters.
        inverted, options: String.CompareOptions.literal,
        range: nil) != nil {
            return nil
        }

        self.init(capacity: hexString.count / 2)

        for i in stride(from: 0, to: hexString.count, by: 2) {
            let startIndex = hexString.index(hexString.
            startIndex, offsetBy: i)
            let endIndex = hexString.index(hexString.
            startIndex, offsetBy: i + 1)
            let hexPair = String(hexString[startIndex...
            endIndex])
            let num = UInt8(hexPair, radix: 16)!
            self.append(num)
        }
    }

    var hexString: String {
        map { String(format: "%02hhx", $0) }.joined()
    }
}
```

Please note that the initializer is optional as not every String can be converted to Data. We also used force unwrapping because we made all the necessary checks in advance and we know that converting hexPair to UInt8 will never fail.

The following example converts a hex-encoded "Swift" string to readable text.

```
let hexSwift = "5377696674"
let hexData = Data(hexString: hexSwift)!
let hexString = String(data: hexData, encoding: .utf8)!
print(hexString)
```

Similarly, these conversions can be presented as String extensions (Recipe 3-10):

Recipe 3-10. Converting Hex String to Data and Back (As String Extensions)

```
public extension String {
    init(hexFromData: Data) {
        append(contentsOf: hexFromData.map { String(format:
        "%02hhx", $0) }.joined())
    }

    func hexToData() -> Data? {
        if hexString.count % 2 != 0 {
            return nil
        }

        let allowedCharacters = CharacterSet(charactersIn:
        "01234567890abcdefABCDEF")
        if hexString.rangeOfCharacter(from: allowedCharacters.
        inverted, options: String.CompareOptions.literal,
        range: nil) != nil {
            return nil
        }
```

```
    var result = Data(capacity: self.count / 2)

    for i in stride(from: 0, to: hexString.count, by: 2) {
        let startIndex = hexString.index(hexString.
        startIndex, offsetBy: i)
        let endIndex = hexString.index(hexString.
        startIndex, offsetBy: i + 1)
        let hexPair = String(hexString[startIndex...
        endIndex])
        let num = UInt8(hexPair, radix: 16)!
        result.append(num)
    }

    return result
  }
}
```

MD5, SHA, and Other Hashes

Hashes are useful when you need to convert data into a short string without the possibility to restore the original data. Hashes can't be restored, but they can be compared. The same data always produces the same hash.

One of the most popular use cases is storing passwords. As you probably know, websites and apps that require registration never send you your password when you try to restore it – they offer to create a new one instead. It works this way because they don't store your password as it's unsafe. What they do is to store a hash of your password. When you type the same password during the next login, their hashes match, and the server returns a successful response. Said response is usually a session token. If you made a mistake at least in one character, the hash will be different, and the server will return an error. There's a tiny chance that hashes will match, but it's so small that we can ignore it.

Note   An MD5 hash is 128 bits long (16 bytes). It means there are 2^{128} unique hashes. The chance that two hashes will be accidentally the same is $1/2^{128}$, which is around $3 * 10^{-39}$, or $3 * 10^{-37}$%, or 0.0000000000003 yoctopercent.

Another common use of hashes is data verification. If you send a big portion of data (one song in an mp3 format contains millions of bytes), you may want to make sure it safely reaches the other end. The stack or protocols we use on the Internet guarantee it for us – they use hashes and control sequences under the hood. But sometimes, we need to verify the data ourselves. For example, to confirm that the data was downloaded completely after the app crashed or was terminated to save battery. For this purpose, we can calculate the hash of a file in advance and store it on a server. On an app side, we calculate the hash of a downloaded file; then we compare them. If hashes match, very likely it's the same data. And as a hash is only 16 bytes long (in the case of MD5), it's not a big trouble to verify it.

Now let's see how we can calculate hashes, starting with the most popular one – MD5.

MD5 Hash

MD5 (message-digest algorithm, version 5) was originally used in cryptography, but nowadays, it has found usages in other areas. Cryptography, on the other hand, stopped widely using it because of its extensive vulnerabilities.

Any data can be encoded, but more often than not, it comes to `Data` and `String` objects. `String` needs to be converted to `Data` before a hash calculation can be made. The result is always a `Data` object, which can be printed using hex or Base64 representation.

127

Swift doesn't provide native MD5 hashing implementation, but we can use the CommonCrypto library. Remember that if you're using a production app, not a playground, you need to create a bridging header and include a CommonCrypto header:

```
#import <CommonCrypto/CommonCrypto.h>
```

Moreover, if you test the following code, you may get this warning:

```
'CC_MD5' was deprecated in iOS 13.0: This function is
cryptographically broken and should not be used in security
contexts. Clients should migrate to SHA256 (or stronger).
```

This means that Swift considers MD5 algorithm not suitable for cryptographic purposes, but it's ok to use for data validation. As for SHA-256 and other algorithms, we'll go over them later in this chapter. Recipe 3-11 shows how to calculate MD5 hash of Data and String.

Recipe 3-11. Calculating an MD5 Hash

```swift
import var CommonCrypto.CC_MD5_DIGEST_LENGTH
import func CommonCrypto.CC_MD5
import typealias CommonCrypto.CC_LONG

public extension String {
    var md5: Data? {
        data(using: .utf8)?.md5
    }
}

public extension Data {
    var md5: Data {
        let length = Int(CC_MD5_DIGEST_LENGTH)
        var hash = Data(count: length)

        _ = hash.withUnsafeMutableBytes { digestBytes ->
        UInt8 in
```

```
        self.withUnsafeBytes { messageBytes -> UInt8 in
            if let messageBytesBaseAddress = messageBytes.
            baseAddress, let digestBytesBlindMemory =
            digestBytes.bindMemory(to: UInt8.self).
            baseAddress {
                let messageLength = CC_LONG(self.count)
                CC_MD5(messageBytesBaseAddress,
                messageLength, digestBytesBlindMemory)
            }
            return 0
        }
    }
    return hash
    }
}
```

The preceding extension allows us to calculate MD5 hashes of both String and Data objects. In order to calculate a String hash, it gets a UTF-8 representation of it.

Note   Even though it's a function, and not the simplest one, we present it as a computed property because, first, it doesn't change the original object and, second, it's a property or characteristic of it.

If your app targets iOS 13 or later, you can use CryptoKit as shown in Recipe 3-12.

Recipe 3-12. Calculating MD5 Using CryptoKit (iOS 13 or Later)

```
import CryptoKit

public extension Data {
    var md5: Data {
```

```
        let bytes = Insecure.MD5.hash(data: self).map { $0
        as UInt8 }
        return Data(bytes: bytes, count: bytes.count)
    }
}
```

These two implementations return identical results. The difference is that the first one works in older versions of iOS while the second one is much shorter and clearer. It's recommended to migrate to a new algorithm as soon as you drop support of iOS 12 and earlier.

Note   This extension doesn't generate a warning, but it has the word "Insecure" in it. It should give the developer an idea that the usage of this function must be limited.

SHA Hashes

As we discussed earlier, MD5 is not suitable for security purposes. It's too fast and easy. A good solution for password storing and other security purposes is using hashes from the SHA group. SHA stands for Secure Hash Algorithm. There are many algorithms in this group, but the most common ones are SHA-1 and SHA-256.

SHA-1 produces a 160-bit hash. Known since 1995, it's considered not to be safe enough, yet much safer than MD5.

SHA-256 is a variant of the SHA-2 algorithm. It produces a 256-bit hash. It provides a good balance between performance and security, and it is recommended for security purposes. Calculation of SHA-1, SHA-256 and SHA-512 from Data and String is shown in Recipe 3-13.

Recipe 3-13. Calculating SHA Hashes

```
public extension String {
    var sha1: Data? {
        data(using: .utf8)?.sha1
    }

    var sha256: Data? {
        data(using: .utf8)?.sha256
    }

    var sha512: Data? {
        data(using: .utf8)?.sha512
    }
}

public extension Data {
    var sha1: Data {
        let bytes = Insecure.SHA1.hash(data: self).map { $0
        as UInt8 }
        return Data(bytes: bytes, count: bytes.count)
    }

    var sha256: Data {
        let bytes = SHA256.hash(data: self).map { $0 as UInt8 }
        return Data(bytes: bytes, count: bytes.count)
    }

    var sha512: Data {
        let bytes = SHA512.hash(data: self).map { $0 as UInt8 }
        return Data(bytes: bytes, count: bytes.count)
    }
}
```

As you can see, since SHA-256, the insecure prefix disappears.
Similarly, you can implement other algorithms.

Hashable Protocol and Swift Hashes

Swift offers its own hashing functionality. Any class, struct, or other language construct conforming to the Hashable protocol can be hashed. This functionality is used for `Dictionary` and `Set`. Instead of storing keys, Swift stores hashes. The Hashable protocol has a function `hash(into:)`:

```
func hash(into hasher: inout Hasher) {
    hasher.combine(property1)
    hasher.combine(property2)
    // ... other properties
}
```

You don't usually need to implement this function. If all members of your class or struct are hashable, you only need to declare conformance to the `Hashable` protocol.

`Hashable` classes should be also equatable (conforming to the `Equatable` protocol). It means that they should declare a function to check the equality of the two instances.

Note   Swift offers two different operators: == and ===. The first one is equality, and this operator is required to conform to the Equatable protocol. The second one is the identity operator, and it compares memory addresses of two classes. If two equatable classes are identical, it means they're also equal, but if they're equal, it doesn't guarantee that they're identical.

The algorithm under the hood of Swift `Hasher` is not the same in different Swift versions. We don't need to know which exact algorithm is used; for us, that's an abstraction. Trying to use the specifics of class implementation will cause problems if new versions of Swift change implementation again.

What's more, generated hashes should never be used outside an app, or even stored somewhere. They're used for comparing keys in structures like Set or Dictionary only. To send a hash to a server, you need to use one of the standard algorithms, like SHA or MD5.

Salt

As we discussed password hashing earlier, it's important to give a mention to *salt*. Not the widespread seasoning, but the string or two of code that an app adds to the beginning and/or end of your password before hash calculation. Salt must be the same and shouldn't change in new versions of an app.

Salt helps to keep your password private. If two different services use SHA-256 to store passwords, the same password will generate the same SHA-256, which will create a vulnerability. The server administrator will be able to use your password hash to log in to another service. Using salt is pretty straightforward. You can see how to use it in Recipe 3-14.

Note   It's not recommended to use the same password for two different services, but as a developer, you should always assume that users will ignore this recommendation.

Recipe 3-14. Calculating the Hash of a Password

```
let password = "..."
let leftSalt = "..." // String constant, which should be the
same in all versions of your app
let rightSalt = "..." // String constant, which should be the
same in all versions of your app
let saltedPassword = "\(leftSalt)\(password)\(rightSalt)"
let passwordHash = saltedPassword.sha256
```

This is a safe way to send a password to the server. On its side, the server script can add another salt and calculate another password hash.

While developing a security system, be creative. Add unexpected layers of protection. Hackers know perfectly well everything described here. Do more. Use a combination of different methods to confuse them and to stay one step ahead.

Integer Indexing

Swift doesn't accept integer numbers as `String` indexes. For example, you can't just get the 5th `Character` of a `String`. Apple explains it with internal encoding. As characters may have different lengths, indexing them with Int, like in C, may create confusion and index not a 5th character, but a 5th byte or 5th pair of bytes.

Unlike `Int`, `String.Index` gives context. Belonging to a particular `String`, it knows which `Character` it refers to and knows how *wide* it is.

In real life, we often need to get n-th letter in word or range with known indices like in our Recipe 3-9 in Section "Hex encoding", converting hex `String` to `Data`.

The `String` extensions we'll write in this section will add functionality to get a `Character` or a `Substring` from a `String` using Int-based subscripts or ranges.

Before we move on, there's one detail that needs some attention. Swift allows two different structures: `String` and `Substring`. While `String` actually stores text data, `Substring` is only a reference to an existing `String`.

`Substring` can be easily converted to `String`:

```
let substring: Substring = ...
let string: String = String(substring)
```

At the same time, if you actively work with substrings, you may want to use `StringProtocol` in your functions instead of `String`. It will allow you to pass both `String` and `Substring`. If you don't modify it, there's no difference; you won't need to convert one into another. But that decision has a price as well – when you turn a `Substring` into a `String`, Swift copies all the data into a new memory fragment. It may not be important if you do it once or twice with short strings, but if you need an efficient app, you need to keep this in mind.

Recipe 3-15 shows how to add integer indexing to Strings in your project, but first let's decide what we want:

```
let str = "Some string"
let substring = str[5...] // "string" word wrapped into
                             Substring object
let firstChar = substring[0] // Character "S"
```

Recipe 3-15. Integer Indexing of Strings

```
public extension String {
    subscript (i: Int) -> Character {
        return self[index(startIndex, offsetBy: i)]
    }

    subscript (bounds: CountableRange<Int>) -> Substring {
        let start = index(startIndex, offsetBy: bounds.
        lowerBound)
        let end = index(startIndex, offsetBy: bounds.
        upperBound)
        if end < start { return "" }
        return self[start..<end]
    }
}
```

```
subscript (bounds: CountableClosedRange<Int>) ->
Substring {
    let start = index(startIndex, offsetBy: bounds.
    lowerBound)
    let end = index(startIndex, offsetBy: bounds.
    upperBound)
    if end < start { return "" }
    return self[start...end]
}

subscript (bounds: CountablePartialRangeFrom<Int>) ->
Substring {
    let start = index(startIndex, offsetBy: bounds.
    lowerBound)
    let end = index(endIndex, offsetBy: -1)
    if end < start { return "" }
    return self[start...end]
}

subscript (bounds: PartialRangeThrough<Int>) -> Substring {
    let end = index(startIndex, offsetBy: bounds.upperBound)
    if end < startIndex { return "" }
    return self[startIndex...end]
}

subscript (bounds: PartialRangeUpTo<Int>) -> Substring {
    let end = index(startIndex, offsetBy: bounds.upperBound)
    if end < startIndex { return "" }
    return self[startIndex..<end]
}
}
```

Localization

iOS has its own localization system. It automatically chooses the preferred language based on the user's settings and localizes both storyboards and strings in the source code if you provide a localization for them.

NSLocalizedString Macro

To get a localized version of a string in the source code, you should use a macro:

```
NSLocalizedString(key, comment)
```

It's available in any part of an iOS app. A key argument is an identifier of a string. Identifiers should be unique, and they can contain any symbol allowed in a Swift `String` object. A comment is used for generating files for translators. It's allowed to keep it empty if you're not generating a translation file with Xcode or `genstrings` utility.

Files with Translations

You should add files with a `strings` extension – for example, `Localised.strings` to provide a translation. You can either put them manually in directories corresponding to languages or do it using Xcode.

A strings file is a simple text file with key-value pairs. Pairs are separated with a semicolon. Key and value are separated with an equal sign. Both keys and values should be inside quotation marks:

```
"firstName": "First Name";
```

To avoid confusion, we use more precise identifiers, for example:

```
"auth.firstName.title": "First Name";
"auth.firstName.placeholder": "Enter your first name here";
```

LocalizedStringKey Struct

Localization in SwiftUI is usually done with LocalizedStringKey. It's a struct, but it also conforms to protocol ExpressibleByStringLiteral, which means that we can assign a String to it.

```
let name: LocalizedStringKey = "name"
let text = Text(name)
```

Text in this code will get a value from translation.

LocalizedStringKey also conforms to ExpressibleByStringInterpolation. You can use it with \() construction.

```
let name = "Alex"
Text("hello \(name)")
```

Translation file should contain

```
"hello %@" = "Hello %@!";
```

Text view will be created with string "Hello Alex!".

Syntactic Sugar

When you have a lot of localizable content, it can be annoying to type NSLocalizedString every time. Wouldn't it look much better with an extension from Recipe 3-16?

Recipe 3-16. Localized Strings

```
public extension StringProtocol {
    var localised: String {
        NSLocalizedString(self, "")
    }
}
```

Now you can use it this way:

```
label.text = "auth.firstName.title".localised
```

Note UI elements from storyboards or nibs can be localized without writing code. Mark a storyboard or nib file as localizable in Xcode Interface Builder. Xcode will generate the necessary files automatically, you'll only need to change texts.

Summary

Old programming languages like C didn't have a special type for strings, programmers used array of bytes to store them. It created a lot of potential bugs in code and made string analysis nearly impossible. Swift with its String type and extensions offers completely different approach.

In this chapter we saw how to check if a String has letters or digits, it has contains valid name, email or other data. We used String for storing hashes, verifying data and encrypting passwords. Finally, we talked about localization of iOS apps.

Until now we were discussing data processing, but didn't discuss presentation. In the next chapter we'll fix it and talk about user interface.

CHAPTER 4

UIKit and Storyboards

For many years, UIKit was the only way to implement user interfaces in iOS apps, and storyboards mechanism was the main tool to make layouts. Recently, SwiftUI was introduced, which is a logical part of the transition from Objective-C to native Swift-only code. But UIKit still plays an important role in iOS development.

First of all, there's a lot of legacy code. Many apps and frameworks started long before the moment SwiftUI was introduced. The most popular iOS libraries gained developers' trust for years, and we're not ready to stop using them and make a full transition to SwiftUI.

Secondly, SwiftUI was introduced only in iOS 13.0, macOS 10.15, etc. If your app needs to support iOS 12, which makes sense, at least for now, you can't use SwiftUI.

Thirdly, UIKit elements can be integrated into SwiftUI code. If you found a cool good-looking UI library on GitHub, but it's written on UIKit, and your app uses SwiftUI, that's not a reason not to use it. We'll look into it in details in the chapter about SwiftUI.

And now let's see how can we get the most out of UIKit and iOS storyboards.

Navigation Between App Screens

Each iOS application has more than one screen. Web developers often call them pages, so many iOS developers started to do the same. Still, there are differences between app screens and web pages. At the same time, modern

© Alexander Nekrasov 2022
A. Nekrasov, *Swift Recipes for iOS Developers*,
https://doi.org/10.1007/978-1-4842-8098-0_4

devices started to offer split-screen view, which makes mobile apps use only part of the device screen and use devices with external screens. In iOS 13.0, Apple introduced the conception of Scenes. Each scene can have one or more windows and contain one or more view controllers. Confusing, right? Let's dive into it.

Screens, Windows, and Views

If you have an iOS device, you have a screen. A screen is represented by a `UIScreen` object. The main screen is a singleton; you can access it from any part of your app. If you're writing a one-screen app, you can assume that there's nothing else.

`UIScreen` has a `UIWindow` object. It's a visible window. The term *window* comes from desktop development. We all know the Windows operating system, which uses *window* as a core concept. Unlike desktop operating systems, in iOS, a `UIWindow` doesn't have border or decorations.

`UIWindow` was created to show user interface, and user interface consists of *views*. One of them is a root view. This root view shows one *app screen* or *app page* as web developers would say. In UIKit, it's controlled by `UIViewController`, `UINavigationController`, or other controller.

These controllers have other controllers or views inside. This way, we get a tree-style hierarchy of views and controllers.

Navigation in iOS Apps

UIKit offers two main ways to navigate:

- Modal presentation of new elements

- Pushing elements with `UINavigationController`

Note   Tab-based navigation is common in mobile apps. The tab model in iOS is a controller UITabBarController, with up to five child controllers. We'll leave them beyond the scope.

The element here is one of the controllers, usually the UIViewController.

UIViewController contains a tree of UIView objects of its subclasses. One of them is a root UIView, while the other ones are inside it, directly or through other objects.

When we talk about navigation in iOS apps, we usually mean switching from one UIViewController to another (Figure 4-1). When you have UINavigationController, you can push a new controller to a navigation stack:

```
pushViewController(_:animated:)
```

When you present it modally, you do it with the following method:

```
present(_:animated:completion:)
```

What's the difference?

Besides visual effects, there's a significant difference in logic. When you use UINavigationController, you have a navigation stack, and you can pop back to any of the previously pushed elements. You can also add an element to a stack, change order, and do many other operations.

When you present a modal element, you can only dismiss it. You don't have access to the whole stack, and you can't dismiss several elements at a time. But it's useful regardless. Imagine that you're writing an app for food ordering. The user browses the menu, adds things to the cart, and then opens the cart. This is the case when it makes sense to use a modal presentation. But instead of UIViewController, we present

`UINavigationController`, which has `UIViewController` elements with purchase flow. When the user finishes their purchase, you go back to the menu by dismissing the model element.

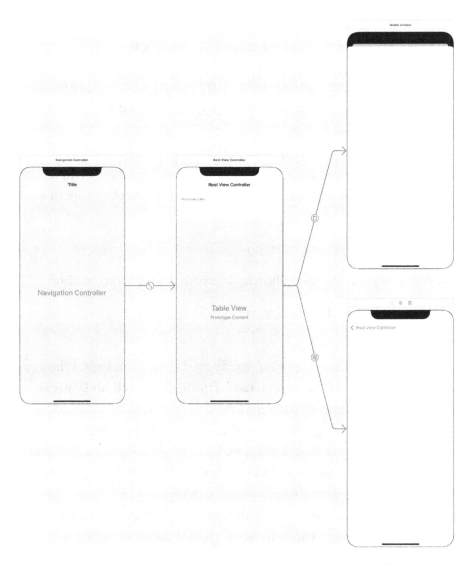

Figure 4-1. *Navigation in an iOS app. Navigation controller, root controller, and view controllers with modal and push presentation (left to right)*

Besides these two methods of showing another screen, you can use, for example, a replacement. If you have a loading screen, we don't want to keep it in the navigation stack or in the memory "behind" the active UI. We simply want to replace it. We'll see how to do that later.

The last important concept is dialog or popover presentation. Logically, it's the same as modal presentation, but instead of replacing the screen behind, it shows it on top of it. Take your iPhone or iPad, tap any of the apps on Home Screen and hold. You'll see a menu. It's an example of popover presentation.

Scenes

Since iOS 13, Apple introduces *Scenes*. And if in the beginning using scenes was optional, Xcode 12 doesn't give a choice anymore. You still can delete all the code related to scenes and use it the old-fashioned way, but probably in the future, that won't be an option anymore.

Note   Despite the fact that scenes were introduced together with SwiftUI, they're used in UIKit as well.

Scenes offer `UIWindowScene` objects, which control the windows and view controllers in your app. Basically, it's a way to make a multi-window app. Each scene must have a delegate – a `UIWindowSceneDelegate` object, but they don't have to be different. You can use one delegate for multiple scenes. Scenes share app memory and other resources.

We will leave multiwindow apps behind the scope, but using scenes changes the way we access `UIWindow` and handle app life cycle; that's why it's important to know how to use scenes.

Going Back

Storyboards allow us to create controllers, view controllers, and segues to go from one app screen to another. They allow us to choose the presentation method and set up the transition animation, but they don't allow us to do such a simple thing as going back.

Depending on the way you switched to your current view controller, going back can be done with one of these two ways:

```
dismiss(animated:, completion:)
// and
navigationController?.popViewController(animated:)
```

In both cases, we need to create an @IBAction function and connect it to a button. And this function should be the same in all view controllers – or almost the same. What if we write a function (Recipe 4-1) that will go back exactly to a previous element, no matter if it was presented modally or pushed with UINavigationController?

Recipe 4-1. Going Back to a Previous Screen

```swift
public extension UIViewController {
    @IBAction func goBack() {
        if let nc = navigationController,
           nc.viewControllers.count >= 2 {
            nc.popViewController(animated: true)
        } else {
            dismiss(animated: true, completion: nil)
        }
    }
}
```

First of all, we check if this `UIViewController` is inside `UINavigationController`. If yes, it has a non-nil `navigationController` property. In this case, we need to check if it's a root `UIViewController` in that `UINavigationController`. If it's a root, we can't pop; it will be simply ignored. We need to dismiss it. If `navigationController` is `nil`, it means that it was never inside the `UINavigationController` stack, and we can only dismiss it.

Written as a `UIViewController` extension, this function will be available for all view controllers in the app. If you have a simple "About" screen, which doesn't have any logic, you won't even need to create a subclass of `UIViewController` for it.

Note   This recipe doesn't work inside more complex controllers like UITabController. If you need to go to a previous tab when the user taps a back button, you'll have to create your own stack.

Replacing Root View

Another typical situation that we discussed previously is replacing. If you don't need a screen and all the previous screens before it, you can instantiate a new view controller and show it as root.

In a standard iOS app, there's `AppDelegate` class. Xcode creates it automatically when you start a new project. Depending on the configuration, `AppDelegate` may have a window property, or this property may be in the `SceneDelegate` class.

When you have a reference to a `UIWindow` object, you can replace the root view controller like shown in Recipe 4-2:

Recipe 4-2. Replacing a Root View Controller

```
public extension UIWindow {
    func replaceRootViewController(with viewController:
UIViewController) {
        rootViewController = viewController
        makeKeyAndVisible()
    }
}
```

The challenge here is to get a window. In old-style projects, we have a window as a property of `UIApplication`. Luckily, `UIApplication` in a project with scenes has another property – connectedScenes. Some of these "connected scenes" are of `UIWindowScene` type. From `UIWindowScene`, we can extract a reference to a `UIWindow` object (Recipes 4-3 through 4-5).

Recipe 4-3. Getting Main UIWindow in Projects with scenes

```
@available(iOS 13.0, *)
public extension UIApplication {
    var currentWindow: UIWindow? {
        connectedScenes
            .filter {$0.activationState == .foregroundActive}
            .compactMap { $0 as? UIWindowScene }
            .first?
            .windows
            .first(where: { $0.isKeyWindow })
    }
}
```

In a project without scenes, you can get it easier.

Recipe 4-4. Getting Main UIWindow in Projects without scenes

```
public extension UIWindow {
    static var main: UIWindow? {
        (UIApplication.shared.delegate as? AppDelegate)?.window
    }
}
```

Note   This recipe assumes that your app has the AppDelegate class, which implements the UIApplicationDelegate protocol and is a main delegate of your app.

And finally, we can wrap up all these methods up into one static function in a UIWindow extension.

Recipe 4-5. Replacing Root View Controller (Static)

```
public extension UIWindow {
    static func replaceMainRootViewController(with
    viewController: UIViewController) -> Bool {
        var window: UIWindow?
        if #available(iOS 13, *) {
            window = UIApplication.shared.currentWindow
        } else {
            window = UIWindow.main
        }

        window?.replaceRootViewController(with: viewController)
        return window != nil
    }
}
```

The function `replaceMainRootViewController` replaces the root view controller in the main window if it exists. If the window doesn't exist or the function can't find it, it returns false, otherwise – true.

Modifying UINavigationController Stack

Let's say you have a long sequence of screens where the user chooses something. For example, the user is presented with a test. They can submit questions or skip them. If they submit a question, it disappears forever; otherwise, it stays in the stack so they can come back and answer it later.

Let's see a different example. The user is ordering furniture. They choose the configuration, color, and all the details. Finally, the user pays for it, and since this moment, we don't want to let them go back to configuring their purchase. We want to show the order tracking. But we don't want to clear the whole stack – when the user taps on the back button, they should go back to the section of the app they'd used before, but the ordering flow should disappear until they make a new order.

One more situation – adding a new screen. For example, we may want to warn the user that if they go back, their order will be cancelled. We don't want them to get stuck on a screen; otherwise, they'll just "kill" the app. But we need to warn them that the ordering process is not finished and they should finish it before going back. It can be done with a popup, but designers may have another opinion.

We'll have a look at the following cases:

- Removing unnecessary `UIViewController`s from the stack

- Returning the user to a specific `UIViewController` in the stack

- Adding `UIViewController` to the stack

As we discussed before, when UIViewController is a part of the navigation stack, it has the non-nil property navigationController. This navigationController has a very important property – viewController. This property contains the navigation stack – a list of UIViewController objects starting with a root element.

Note   When you access navigationController?.viewControllers from UIViewController, it always contains self.

Removing Elements from the Navigation Stack

Let's suppose that the user finished a flow which we don't want them to go back to, but we still allow returning to the view controllers preceding that flow. As unnecessary elements of the stack are always part of our app and always known, we know the class names of those elements. Recipe 4-6 shows how to remove unnecessary elements from navigation stack using filter method.

Recipe 4-6.   Removing Elements of a Known Type from the Navigation Stack

```
public extension UINavigationController {
    func removeElements<T: UIViewController>(of type: T.Type) {
        viewControllers = viewControllers.filter {
            !($0 is T)
        }
    }
}
```

Usage

```
navigationController?.removeElements(of:
UnnecessaryViewController.self)
```

151

I advise you not to remove the current front view controller this way. If you need to remove it, use `navigationController?.popViewController(animated:)` or the `goBack` function from the beginning of this chapter instead. Also, it's better to modify a stack when the front view controller is fully presented on the screen. It should be either in the `viewDidAppear(animated:)` function or later.

Returning the User to a Specific View Controller

Imagine that you're starting a new game, and the first thing you need to do is to create your own character. You choose their body, their face, color of their hair, the shape of their nose, and... you end up not liking it at all! You can go back to the previous step or start over. This "start over" function is an example of navigation to a specific view controller.

Like in the previous recipe, we'll identify the view controller by its class, and as a matter of fact, it should be a subclass of `UIViewController`. All view controllers between a chosen one and a front one should be removed from the stack as shown in Recipe 4-7.

Recipe 4-7. Returning the User to a Specific View Controller

```
public extension UINavigationController {
    func returnToElement<T: UIViewController>(of type: T.Type,
    animated: Bool) -> Bool {
        guard let lastIndex = viewControllers.lastIndex(where:
        { $0 is T }) else {
            return false
        }

        if viewControllers[lastIndex] == viewControllers.last {
            return false
        }
```

```
        viewControllers.removeSubrange(lastIndex.advanced
        (by: 1)..<viewControllers.endIndex.advanced(by: -1))
        popViewController(animated: animated)
        return true
    }
}
```

Usage

```
navigationController?.returnToElement(of: StartViewController.
self, animated: true)
```

If you want to return to the beginning of a stack, you can use a standard method:

```
navigationController?.popToRootViewController(animated: true)
```

Popups and Dialogs

Popup windows with information or question are very common for user interface (Figures 4-2, 4-3 and 4-4). iOS offers us UIAlertController to show a popup, but it takes three lines of code to show a simple message. For something more complex, we need to write more code. When we have multiple branches of code verifying data and showing error messages, creating and setting up UIAlertController in each of them is not *DRY*.

Showing Alerts, Errors, and Warnings

Apart from shorter and cleaner code, these functions are useful if you want to use custom styles in the future. Instead of replacing standard popups in the whole project, you'll have them all in one place. Recipe 4-8 shows simple extensions of UIViewController showing alert dialog.

Figure 4-2. *Error dialog*

Recipe 4-8. Showing Simple Popups

```
public extension UIViewController {
    func show(error: String) {
        let alert = UIAlertController(title: "Error", message:
        error, preferredStyle: .alert)
        alert.addAction(UIAlertAction(title: "OK", style:
        .cancel, handler: nil))
        present(alert, animated: true, completion: nil)
    }

    func show(warning: String) {
        let alert = UIAlertController(title: "Warning",
        message: warning, preferredStyle: .alert)
        alert.addAction(UIAlertAction(title: "OK", style:
        .cancel, handler: nil))
        present(alert, animated: true, completion: nil)
    }
}
```

These popups are written as a `UIViewController` extension. It's the most common place to call them. They don't give any feedback, just show a popup. If your app is localized to more than one language, you can change hard-coded strings like "`Error`" or "`OK`" with localized versions.

If you're inside `UIViewController`, you can call them this way:

```
let error: Error // Error from API call
self.show(error: error.localizedDescription)
```

Don't forget that you must be in the main thread. If you're not sure, modify these functions to make sure you're always in the main thread.

Asking General Questions

A general question (also known as a polar question) is a question with two possible answers – positive or negative. Usually, it's "yes" or "no". "Are you sure you want to quit?" "Overwrite this file?" "Couldn't connect. Would you like to reenter the password?" ... Sounds familiar? They're all popups with general questions. Recipe 4-9 shows how to make a function asking such a question and called with a single line of code.

Figure 4-3. *Confirm dialog*

Recipe 4-9. General Question Popup

```
public extension UIViewController {
    func ask(title: String?, question: String?,
    positiveButtonTitle: String = "Yes", negativeButtonTitle:
    String = "No", isDangerousAction: Bool = false, delegate: @
    escaping (_ agreed: Bool) -> Void) {
```

155

```
    let alert = UIAlertController(title: title, message:
    question, preferredStyle: .alert)
    alert.addAction(UIAlertAction(title:
    positiveButtonTitle, style: isDangerousAction ?
    .destructive : .default) { (_) in
        delegate(true)
    })
    alert.addAction(UIAlertAction(title:
    negativeButtonTitle, style: .cancel) { (_) in
        delegate(false)
    })
    present(alert, animated: true, completion: nil)
  }
}
```

Asking Questions with a One-Line String Answer

Another typical popup is a dialog asking a simple question with a text answer. For example, if you join a network, it can ask for a password. It must always have two buttons – "OK" and "Cancel". Recipe 4-10 shows how to write such a dialog as UIViewController extension.

Figure 4-4. *Text entry dialog*

Recipe 4-10. Simple Text Question Popup

```
public extension UIViewController {
    func ask(title: String?, question: String?, placeholder:
    String?, keyboardType: UIKeyboardType = .default, delegate:
    @escaping (_ answer: String?) -> Void) {
        let alert = UIAlertController(title: title, message:
        question, preferredStyle: .alert)
        alert.addTextField { (textField) in
            textField.placeholder = placeholder
            textField.keyboardType = keyboardType
        }
        alert.addAction(UIAlertAction(title: "OK", style:
        .default) { (_) in
            let answer = alert.textFields?.first?.text
            delegate(answer)
        })
        alert.addAction(UIAlertAction(title: "Cancel", style:
        .cancel) { (_) in
            delegate(nil)
        })
        present(alert, animated: true, completion: nil)
    }
}
```

Picking Date and Time

In Chapter 2, we discussed the validation of user form and decided that the best solution for dates is to show a date picker. We can show it in place of an on-screen keyboard or show a popup.

Is it possible to add `UIDatePicker` to `UIAlertView`? Yes, but it's not a good idea. The problem is that `UIAlertView` doesn't have a component stack; it can natively contain `UILabel` and `UITextField`. The size of `UIAlertView` is calculated based on the size of these components. `UIView` can have children, so you *can* add other `UIView` subclasses to it, but there's no guarantee it will fit well.

Recipe 4-11 shows how to create a completely custom popup and add it on top of your layout. How to request this popup is shown in Recipe 4-12. To create a layout using the Auto Layout feature, we'll use the SnapKit framework available on GitHub: `https://github.com/SnapKit/SnapKit`.

What Is SnapKit?

SnapKit is a popular and well-maintained library allowing you to create layouts programmatically, without storyboards or nibs, but also without manually adding every single constraint with a long line of code. Basically, this library just adds syntactic sugar to constraint-making code.

For example, this code snippet from the official SnapKit website creates a green box and adds it to root view.

```
import SnapKit

class MyViewController: UIViewController {

    lazy var box = UIView()

    override func viewDidLoad() {
        super.viewDidLoad()

        self.view.addSubview(box)
        box.backgroundColor = .green
        box.snp.makeConstraints { (make) -> Void in
            make.width.height.equalTo(50)
```

```
        make.center.equalTo(self.view)
      }
    }
}
```

Date and Time Selector Popup

To get a popup, we need an `UIView` with four children:

- Title label
- Date picker
- OK button
- Cancel button

```
private var frameView: UIView!
private var titleLabel: UILabel!
private var datePicker: UIDatePicker!
private var okButton: UIButton!
private var cancelButton: UIButton!
```

It should have a delegate returning a `Date` object or `nil`.

```
var delegate: (_ date: Date?) -> Void = { _ in }
```

The base class for our popup will be `UIView`. Keep in mind that it can be done differently. We'll just show one example, but you can adjust it to your needs.

Recipe 4-11. Date Picker Popup

```
import SnapKit

public class DatePickerPopup: UIView {
    private var frameView: UIView!
    private var titleLabel: UILabel!
```

```
private var datePicker: UIDatePicker!
private var okButton: UIButton!
private var cancelButton: UIButton!

var delegate: (_ date: Date?) -> Void = { _ in }

var title: String {
    get {
        titleLabel.text ?? ""
    }
    set {
        titleLabel.text = newValue
    }
}

override init(frame: CGRect) {
    super.init(frame: frame)

    commonInit()
}

required init?(coder: NSCoder) {
    super.init(coder: coder)

    commonInit()
}

func commonInit() {
    // Dark shade
    backgroundColor = UIColor(red: 0.0, green: 0.0, blue:
    0.0, alpha: 0.3)

    // Frame view
    frameView = UIView()
    frameView.layer.cornerRadius = 10
```

```
frameView.layer.masksToBounds = true
frameView.backgroundColor = .white
addSubview(frameView)
frameView.snp.makeConstraints { (make) in
    make.center.equalTo(self)
}

// Title label
titleLabel = UILabel()
titleLabel.font = UIFont.systemFont(ofSize: 16,
weight: .bold)
titleLabel.textColor = .black
titleLabel.textAlignment = .center
frameView.addSubview(titleLabel)
titleLabel.snp.makeConstraints { (make) in
    make.top.equalToSuperview().offset(40)
    make.leading.equalToSuperview().offset(40)
    make.trailing.equalToSuperview().offset(-40)
}

// Date picker
datePicker = UIDatePicker()
datePicker.preferredDatePickerStyle = .wheels
datePicker.datePickerMode = .date
datePicker.date = Date()
frameView.addSubview(datePicker)
datePicker.snp.makeConstraints { (make) in
    make.top.equalTo(titleLabel.snp.bottom).offset(20)
    make.leading.equalToSuperview().offset(20)
    make.trailing.equalToSuperview().offset(-20)
}
```

```
    // Buttons
    cancelButton = UIButton()
    cancelButton.setTitle("Cancel", for: .normal)
    cancelButton.setTitleColor(UIColor(red: 0.0, green:
    0.478431, blue: 1.0, alpha: 1.0), for: .normal)
    cancelButton.addTarget(self, action:
    #selector(cancelPressed), for: .touchUpInside)
    okButton = UIButton()
    okButton.setTitle("OK", for: .normal)
    okButton.setTitleColor(UIColor(red: 0.0, green:
    0.478431, blue: 1.0, alpha: 1.0), for: .normal)
    okButton.addTarget(self, action: #selector(okPressed),
    for: .touchUpInside)
    frameView.addSubview(cancelButton)
    frameView.addSubview(okButton)
    cancelButton.snp.makeConstraints { (make) in
        make.top.equalTo(datePicker.snp.bottom)
        make.left.equalToSuperview()
        make.height.equalTo(40)
        make.bottom.equalToSuperview().offset(-40)
    }
    okButton.snp.makeConstraints { (make) in
        make.top.equalTo(datePicker.snp.bottom)
        make.left.equalTo(cancelButton.snp.right)
        make.right.equalToSuperview()
        make.height.equalTo(40)
        make.width.equalTo(cancelButton.snp.width)
    }
}

@objc func cancelPressed() {
    disappearAndReturn(date: nil)
}
```

```swift
@objc func okPressed() {
    disappearAndReturn(date: datePicker.date)
}

private func disappearAndReturn(date: Date?) {
    UIView.animate(withDuration: 0.3) {
        self.alpha = 0.0
    } completion: { (_) in
        self.removeFromSuperview()
        self.delegate(date)
    }
}

static func createAndShow(in viewController:
UIViewController, title: String, delegate: @escaping (_
date: Date?) -> Void) -> DatePickerPopup {
    let popup = DatePickerPopup(frame: viewController.
    view.bounds)
    popup.title = title
    popup.delegate = delegate
    popup.alpha = 0.0
    viewController.view.addSubview(popup)

    UIView.animate(withDuration: 0.3) {
        popup.alpha = 1.0
    }

    return popup
}
}
```

The following extension allows to request this popup inside
UIViewController shorter.

Recipe 4-12. Asking Date from UIViewController

```
public extension UIViewController {
    func askDate(title: String, delegate: @escaping (_ date:
    Date?) -> Void) {
        _ = DatePickerPopup.createAndShow(in: self, title:
        title, delegate: delegate)
    }
}
```

Now, when you have this class, you can ask for a date with one line of code, plus another line to process the result:

```
self.askDate(title: "Date of Birth") { (date) in
    print(date)
}
```

The result will be either a panel with rounded corners (Figure 4-5) in the center of the screen or a central section of the screen. It depends on the screen size of your iPhone.

Figure 4-5. *Date selection dialog*

Date and Time Inside the Bottom Sheet

Showing a popup may be not the best way of asking for date and/or time.
Another way is showing it instead of an on-screen keyboard. If you have a
sequence of UITextFields, it will be more comfortable for the user to see a
date picker in the same place as the keyboard.

This time, it can't be an extension; it needs to be integrated in your
UIViewController or other class, depending on your project architecture.
Recipe 4-13 shows an example of UIViewController subclass showing
date picker instead of keyboard.

Recipe 4-13. Showing Date and Time Picker in a Bottom Sheet

```
public class DateSelectorViewController: UIViewController {
    @IBOutlet weak var tfDOB: UITextField!
    @IBOutlet weak var tfNextField: UITextField!

    var selectedDOB: Date? = nil
```

```swift
let datePicker = UIDatePicker(frame: CGRect(x: 0, y: 0,
width: UIScreen.main.bounds.width, height: 216))

override func viewDidLoad() {
    super.viewDidLoad()

    if #available(iOS 13.4, *) {
        datePicker.preferredDatePickerStyle = .wheels
    }
    datePicker.datePickerMode = .date
    tfDOB.inputView = datePicker
    addDoneButtonOnKeyboard()

    // ...
}

func addDoneButtonOnKeyboard() {
    let doneToolbar: UIToolbar = UIToolbar(frame: CGRect.
    init(x: 0, y: 0, width: UIScreen.main.bounds.width,
    height: 50))
    doneToolbar.barStyle = .default

    let flexSpace = UIBarButtonItem(barButtonSystemItem:
    .flexibleSpace, target: nil, action: nil)
    let done: UIBarButtonItem = UIBarButtonItem(title:
    "Done", style: .done, target: self, action:
    #selector(self.doneButtonAction))

    let items = [flexSpace, done]
    doneToolbar.items = items
    doneToolbar.sizeToFit()

    tfDOB.inputAccessoryView = doneToolbar
}
```

```
@objc func doneButtonAction() {
    tfDOB.text = df.string(from: datePicker.date)
    selectedDOB = datePicker.date
    tfNextField.becomeFirstResponder()
    }
}
```

Maps and Navigation

The iOS platform has a native map framework – MapKit – as well as the preinstalled Maps app that is based on said framework. Writing iOS apps, you can be sure that the user has these tools and you can use them too. Apple Maps is suitable for most cases, but there are alternative map frameworks giving better functionality. Many people prefer Google Maps and Waze for navigation.

In this section, we'll review three situations:

- Showing Apple Map in your app

- Showing Google Maps in your app

- Dynamic navigation using the user's preferred app

Showing Apple Map in an iOS App

Since iOS 3.0, Apple introduced MapKit, which allows you to show a map right in your app as a regular view (see Figure 4-6).

Figure 4-6. *Apple map as a view*

To add a map, open the storyboard (or xib) editor, click the + (plus) button, and choose Map Kit View in the list. Add constraints if you use them and create an outlet. The class name of this view is MKMapView.

```
@IBOutlet weak var mapView: MKMapView!
```

MKMapView is a dynamic component. By default, it allows to interact with the map. If you need it to be static, uncheck User Interaction Enabled.

Note   This property works for all views. If you uncheck User Interaction Enabled (or set isUserInteractionEnabled to false in code), view and its subviews won't respond to user touches and gestures.

In the Map View section in the storyboard/xib editor, you can modify the map type and restrict specific actions, like zoom, scroll, etc.

There are two typical actions you need to do with a map: set position/zoom level and add an *annotation* (also called *pin* and *marker*).

Having latitude and longitude of a point, you can zoom around it:

```
let center = CLLocationCoordinate2D(latitude: latitude,
longitude: longitude)
let region = MKCoordinateRegion(center: center, span:
MKCoordinateSpan(latitudeDelta: 0.01, longitudeDelta: 0.01))
mapView.setRegion(region, animated: true)
```

latitudeDelta and longitudeDelta specify how much space will you see around the center point.

The second typical action is adding a marker (also called a pin):

```
let annotation = MKPointAnnotation()
let centerCoordinate = CLLocationCoordinate2D(latitude:
latitude, longitude: longitude)
annotation.coordinate = centerCoordinate
annotation.title = "Title"
mapView.addAnnotation(annotation)
```

You can add multiple annotations to your map.

To remove an annotation, you can call

```
func removeAnnotations(_ annotations: [MKAnnotation])
```

To remove all annotations, use `mapView.annotations` as an argument.

Showing Google Maps in an iOS App

Unlike Apple Maps, which is included in a set of standard libraries, Google Maps needs to be installed separately, which requires an API key.

If you use CocoaPods as a dependency manager, add it this way:

```
pod 'GoogleMaps'
```

If you prefer not to use CocoaPods, you can download XCFramework from the official website and add it to your project manually. There's no official support of Swift Package Manager. The walkaround is to use a third-party library: `https://github.com/YAtechnologies/GoogleMaps-SP`. It can be added via Swift Package Manager, and it contains the Google Maps framework. Users generally give positive feedback to this library, but whenever possible, it's better to avoid unofficial solutions.

You can get an API key at `https://cloud.google.com`. You need to create an app and follow two more steps:

- Create an API key. You can restrict it, so it can be used only from an iOS app. This way, it can be used only from your app and not any other.

- Enable Maps SDK for iOS.

If you integrated other Google services to the same iOS app, you don't need to create another Google app – you can use the same. For example, if you use Analytics or Crashlytics, your Google app has already been created.

Google Maps is free only within some range. That's why you need to enable billing if you haven't done it earlier. Prices may change within time, but in June 2021, map loads were free, while street views were paid. Even if you're not going to use street views, you should enable billing.

Since this moment, you can add `GMSMapView` to your app. `GMSMapView` is a `UIView` object, which you can add both via storyboards and programmatically.

The map requires an area to show. In case of Google Maps, you need to set up a camera. A `GMSCameraPosition` object specifies latitude, longitude, and zoom.

Let's add a map to our app via storyboard first (Recipe 4-14); then we'll see how to do it programmatically (Recipe 4-15).

In both scenarios, you need to add a key before using maps; otherwise, the app will crash. The best place for it is `AppDelegate`:

```
GMSServices.provideAPIKey("YOUR_API_KEY")
```

Recipe 4-14. Setting Up Map View via Storyboard

```
import GoogleMaps

// Don't forget to call:
// GMSServices.provideAPIKey("YOUR_API_KEY")
// in AppDelegate

class ViewController: UIViewController {
    @IBOutlet var mapView: GMSMapView!

    override func viewDidLoad() {
        super.viewDidLoad()

        let camera = GMSCameraPosition.camera(withLatitude:
        41.6168, longitude: 41.6367, zoom: 6.0)
```

```
        mapView.camera = camera
    }
}
```

Recipe 4-15. Setting Up Map View Programmatically

```
import GoogleMaps

// Don't forget to call:
// GMSServices.provideAPIKey("YOUR_API_KEY")
// in AppDelegate

class ViewController: UIViewController {
    override func viewDidLoad() {
        super.viewDidLoad()
        let camera = GMSCameraPosition.camera(withLatitude:
        41.6168, longitude: 41.6367, zoom: 6.0)
        let mapView = GMSMapView.map(withFrame: self.view.
        frame, camera: camera)
        self.view.addSubview(mapView)
    }
}
```

Google Maps has a great functionality. You can add markers, draw areas, zoom around a specific area, and animate the camera.

The GooglePlaces library provides SDK for working with places and addresses. You can resolve coordinates, search nearby places, and provide other location-aware features.

You can read more about it on the Google Maps Platform portal: https://developers.google.com/maps.

Dynamic Navigation

Let's look closer into a rather typical situation: we have coordinates (latitude and longitude) and a place name. We need to open the user's favorite app to navigate to the desired place (see Figure 4-7). We won't try to integrate navigation inside the app as it's usually not worth it. The Navigation app has many features like navigation in the background, notification, and others, which are not easy to implement.

Figure 4-7. *Choosing an app for navigation*

Each service has a way to start navigation (Recipes 4-16 through 4-18).

Recipe 4-16. Opening Location in Apple Maps

```
let appleURL = "http://maps.apple.com/?daddr=\(latitude),\
(longitude)"
if UIApplication.shared.canOpenURL(appleURL) {
    UIApplication.shared.open(appleURL, options: [:],
    completionHandler: nil)
}
```

Recipe 4-17. Opening Location in Google Maps

```
let googleURL = "comgooglemaps://?daddr=\(latitude),\(longitude
)&directionsmode=driving"
if UIApplication.shared.canOpenURL(googleURL) {
    UIApplication.shared.open(googleURL, options: [:],
    completionHandler: nil)
}
```

Recipe 4-18. Opening Location in Waze

```
let wazeURL = "waze://?ll=\(latitude),\
(longitude)&navigate=false"
if UIApplication.shared.canOpenURL(wazeURL) {
    UIApplication.shared.open(wazeURL, options: [:],
    completionHandler: nil)
}
```

Google and Waze have custom URLs. Recipe 4-19 shows how we can check if they're available in your current system or not.

Recipe 4-19. Universal Navigation

```
public extension UIViewController {
    func openMapButtonAction(latitude: Double, longitude:
    Double) {
```

```swift
let appleURL = "http://maps.apple.com/?daddr=
\(latitude),\(longitude)"
let googleURL = "comgooglemaps://?daddr=\(latitude),
\(longitude)&directionsmode=driving"
let wazeURL = "waze://?ll=\(latitude),
\(longitude)&navigate=false"

let googleItem = ("Google Map", URL(string:googleURL)!)
let wazeItem = ("Waze", URL(string:wazeURL)!)
var installedNavigationApps = [("Apple Maps",
URL(string:appleURL)!)]

if UIApplication.shared.canOpenURL(googleItem.1) {
    installedNavigationApps.append(googleItem)
}

if UIApplication.shared.canOpenURL(wazeItem.1) {
    installedNavigationApps.append(wazeItem)
}

let alert = UIAlertController(title: "Select an
app for navigation", message: nil, preferredStyle:
.actionSheet)
for app in installedNavigationApps {
    let button = UIAlertAction(title: app.0, style:
    .default, handler: { _ in
        UIApplication.shared.open(app.1, options: [:],
        completionHandler: nil)
    })
    alert.addAction(button)
}
let cancel = UIAlertAction(title: "Cancel", style:
.cancel, handler: nil)
```

```
        if let popoverController = alert.
        popoverPresentationController {
            popoverController.sourceView = self.view
        }
        alert.addAction(cancel)
        present(alert, animated: true)
    }
}
```

Rounded Corners, Shadows, and Other Effects

If you use storyboards or nibs for your UI design, you know that it lacks many features. Oftentimes, you need to make some adjustments in the code, which means you need to create an @IBOutlet. And that is uncomfortable.

By adding several extensions, you can fix problems like adding rounded corners, shadows, content cropping, and many others. Figure 4-8 shows how it looks.

Rounded Corners, Content Cropping, and Borders

Rounded corners are a very popular design feature in iOS and macOS apps. Unlike Windows, which becomes more and more square, Apple products get more curves. If you compare Big Sur (macOS 11) with Catalina (macOS 10.15), you'll spot the difference right away.

UIKit has a native way to add rounded corners to basically anything, but it's done implementing it in UILayer, not in UIView. The storyboard editor doesn't have direct access to layers, so you can't add rounded corners there. Recipe 4-20 shows an easy way to fix it.

Recipe 4-20. Rounded Corners

```
public extension UIView {
    @IBInspectable var cornerRadius: CGFloat {
        set { layer.cornerRadius = newValue }
        get { layer.cornerRadius  }
    }
}
```

When you set the corner radius, it will apply to the background, border, and other properties of a layer itself, but not to the content. It won't apply to UIView's children either. If you want to apply rounded corners to everything, you need to set the masksToBounds property. It's a property of a layer. Recipe 4-21 shows how to do it:

Recipe 4-21. Content Cropping

```
public extension UIView {
    @IBInspectable var masksToBounds: Bool {
        set { layer.masksToBounds = newValue }
        get { layer.masksToBounds  }
    }
}
```

Now you can set it directly in the storyboard editor. A word of caution here – it will really apply to everything. For example, if you set it in UIView, all its children will never leave the bounds of the UIView parent.

One of the cases when you may need such behavior is in the root UIView of the UIViewController. When you add a filling background, which may be larger than the root UIView, it will be visible during transition. When you push a new UIViewController to the UINavigationController, it will appear on the right side of the screen (or left in right-to-left layouts). Some out-of-screen elements may be visible. If it's not your desired behavior, set the `maskToBounds` property and its all out-of-screen elements won't be visible during transition.

Before we move on, we'll need another useful extension. The thing is that Swift has two classes: `UIColor` and `CGColor`. `UIColor` is more handy for developers; it gives better access to color components, and it can be exposed to the storyboard editor with the `@IBInspectable` attribute. `CGColor` is more of an internal thing. Even though they both represent color in Swift, they're two different types. Recipe 4-22 converts `CGColor` to `UIColor`.

Recipe 4-22. Converting CGColor to UIColor

```
public extension CGColor {
    var UIColor: UIKit.UIColor {
        return UIKit.UIColor(cgColor: self)
    }
}
```

The extension from Recipe 4-23 allows us to add borders. Borders can have color and width, so we add two properties to the `UIView` class. As in UIKit, all visible elements are subclasses of `UIView`; you can add borders to any of them.

Recipe 4-23. Borders

```
extension UIView {
    @IBInspectable var borderWidth: CGFloat {
        set { layer.borderWidth = newValue }
        get { layer.borderWidth }
    }

    @IBInspectable var borderColor: UIColor? {
        set { layer.borderColor = newValue?.cgColor }
```

```
        get { layer.borderColor?.UIColor }
    }

    @IBInspectable var cornerRadius: CGFloat {
        set { layer.cornerRadius = newValue }
        get { layer.cornerRadius  }
    }

    @IBInspectable var masksToBounds: Bool {
        set { layer.masksToBounds = newValue }
        get { layer.masksToBounds  }
    }
}
```

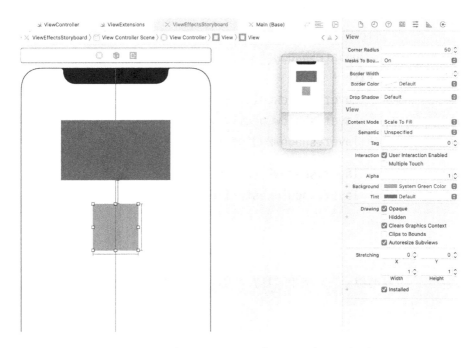

Figure 4-8. *UIView configuration in the storyboard editor*

Shadows

Shadow (Figure 4-9) is a more complex effect, but not because it's hard to implement, but because it must be updated when the layout changes. When iPhone or iPad changes orientation or when elements appear or disappear on a screen, shadow should be re-rendered. Extension adding a shadow to UIView is shown in Recipe 4-24:

Recipe 4-24. Shadows

```
public extension UIView {
    @IBInspectable var dropShadow: Bool {
        set {
            layer.shadowOffset = CGSize(width: 0, height: 0)

            if newValue {
                updateShadow()
            } else {
                layer.shadowColor = UIColor.clear.cgColor
                layer.shadowOpacity = 0.0
                layer.shadowRadius = 0

                layer.shadowPath = nil
                layer.shouldRasterize = false
            }
        }
        get {
            layer.shadowOpacity > 0.0 && layer.shadowRadius > 0
        }
    }
}
```

```swift
func updateShadow() {
    layer.shadowColor = UIColor.black.cgColor
    layer.shadowOpacity = 0.5
    layer.shadowRadius = 4

    layer.shadowPath = UIBezierPath(roundedRect: bounds,
    cornerRadius: layer.cornerRadius).cgPath
    layer.shouldRasterize = true
    layer.rasterizationScale = UIScreen.main.scale
}

func updateShadows() {
    if self.dropShadow {
        self.updateShadow()
    }
    subviews.forEach {
        $0.updateShadows()
    }
}
}
```

Note   Color, radius, and shadow opacity are hard-coded in this
recipe. This is usually the best solution because these parameters are
consistent throughout the app. If you need to make them dynamic,
they can be added as other inspectable properties, and each of them
should trigger an updateShadow function when set.

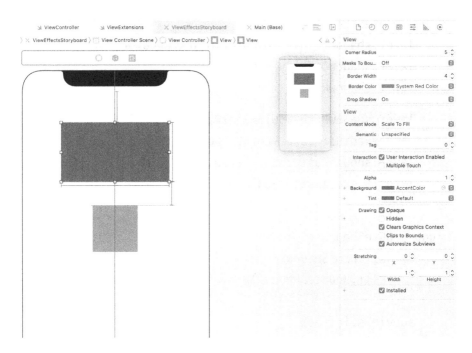

Figure 4-9. *Setting up UIView with shadow, border, and other effects*

This extension offers one inspectable property and two methods. The dropShadow property adds or removes shadow. The updateShadow method creates the shadow using the actual UIView size. For more comfort, there's another method – updateShadows. It updates shadows in UIView and all of its children. You should call it every time the layout changes. A good place for it is the viewDidLayoutSubviews life cycle method of UIViewController.

```
override func viewDidLayoutSubviews() {
    super.viewDidLayoutSubviews()
    view.updateShadows()
}
```

If your UI requires a different configuration of shadows, you can expose all the properties to the storyboard editor. Recipe 4-25 shows how it's done.

Recipe 4-25. Shadows with Properties

```
@IBDesignable
class ShadowView: UIView {
    @IBInspectable var shadowOffset: CGSize {
        get {
            layer.shadowOffset
        }

        set {
            layer.shadowOffset = newValue
        }
    }

    @IBInspectable var shadowColor: UIColor? {
        get {
            if let sc = layer.shadowColor {
                return UIColor(cgColor: sc)
            } else {
                return nil
            }
        }

        set {
            layer.shadowColor = newValue?.cgColor
        }
    }

    @IBInspectable var shadowRadius: CGFloat {
        get {
            layer.shadowRadius
        }

        set {
            layer.shadowRadius = newValue
```

```
        }
    }

    @IBInspectable var shadowOpacity: Float {
        get {
            layer.shadowOpacity
        }

        set {
            layer.shadowOpacity = newValue
        }
    }

    override init(frame: CGRect) {
        super.init(frame: frame)
    }

    required init?(coder: NSCoder) {
        super.init(coder: coder)
    }
}
```

It's a separate class, and if you use both methods in the same project, you shouldn't set the dropShadow property in this ShadowView instance. Instead configure all the parameters individually for the desired result.

UITextField Paddings

One more missing feature of the storyboard editor is adding padding to UITextField elements. Padding may be used for different purposes, starting with better visual appearance and ending with icons and buttons on the sides of the UITextField. At the same time, we often want to keep this space active. When the user taps on it, we want the keyboard to open. Recipe 4-26 shows how to do it.

Recipe 4-26. UITextField padding

```
@IBDesignable
class TextFieldWithPadding: UITextField {

    @IBInspectable var paddingLeft: CGFloat = 0.0
    @IBInspectable var paddingRight: CGFloat = 0.0

    var padding: UIEdgeInsets {
        UIEdgeInsets(top: 0, left: paddingLeft, bottom: 0,
        right: paddingRight)
    }

    required init?(coder aDecoder: NSCoder) {
        super.init(coder: aDecoder)
    }

    override func textRect(forBounds bounds: CGRect) ->
    CGRect {
        bounds.inset(by: padding)
    }

    override func placeholderRect(forBounds bounds: CGRect) ->
    CGRect {
        bounds.inset(by: padding)
    }

    override func editingRect(forBounds bounds: CGRect) ->
    CGRect {
        bounds.inset(by: padding)
    }
}
```

The class `TextFieldWithPadding` offers two extra properties:

- `paddingLeft`
- `paddingRight`

Unfortunately, it has to be a new class, not just an `UITextField` extension, because we need to override the `textRect`, `placeholderRect` and `editingRect` methods.

To use it, simply add `UITextField` in the storyboard editor, change the class to `TextFieldWithPadding` and set `leftPadding` and `rightPadding`.

UITextView placeholder

Unlike `UITextField`, which has a native placeholder, `UITextView` doesn't offer anything like it. It's rather strange, especially assuming that `UITextView` is just a multiline version of `UITextField`. Maybe with some extra features.

Surprisingly, it can be also solved with an extension. But this time, it already exists, we don't need to re-invent it. The library is called UITextView+Placeholder and it's written in Objective-C.

Like `UITextField`, `UITextView` may also need padding. Recipe 4-27 offers a similar extension to add padding to `UITextView` as well.

Recipe 4-27. UITextView padding

```
@IBDesignable
class TextViewWithPadding: UITextView {

    @IBInspectable var paddingLeft: CGFloat = 0.0 {
        didSet {
            updateInsets()
        }
    }
    @IBInspectable var paddingRight: CGFloat = 0.0 {
```

```swift
        didSet {
            updateInsets()
        }
    }
    @IBInspectable var paddingTop: CGFloat = 0.0 {
        didSet {
            updateInsets()
        }
    }
    @IBInspectable var paddingBottom: CGFloat = 0.0 {
        didSet {
            updateInsets()
        }
    }

    required init?(coder aDecoder: NSCoder) {
        super.init(coder: aDecoder)
        updateInsets()
    }

    func updateInsets() {
        textContainerInset = UIEdgeInsets(top: paddingTop,
        left: paddingLeft, bottom: paddingBottom, right:
        paddingRight)
    }
}
```

You can use TextViewWithPadding the same way as TextFieldWith Padding.

Gradients

Another popular design element is gradients. Like in most of the previous cases, gradients can be easily done but can't be done directly from the storyboard editor. And like in previous cases, it's easy to fix.

Our gradient will have the following properties:

- `startColor`

- `endColor`

- `direction.`

In UIKit gradients can be implemented by adding a layer to `UIView`. There's a layer capable of rendering gradients – `CAGradientLayer`.

As it will be a class, not an extension, we can directly override the `layoutSubviews` method to update the gradient when the geometry is changed (Recipe 4-28).

Recipe 4-28. Gradients

```
@IBDesignable
class GradientView: UIView {
    enum Direction: Int {
        case horizontal
        case vertical
    }

    @IBInspectable var startColor: UIColor = .white {
        didSet {
            gradientLayer?.colors = [
                startColor.cgColor,
                endColor.cgColor
            ]
        }
    }
```

```swift
}
@IBInspectable var endColor: UIColor = .black {
    didSet {
        gradientLayer?.colors = [
            startColor.cgColor,
            endColor.cgColor
        ]
    }
}
@IBInspectable var direction: Int = Direction.horizontal.
rawValue {
    didSet {
        if direction == Direction.horizontal.rawValue {
            gradientLayer?.startPoint = CGPoint
            (x: 0.0, y: 0.5)
            gradientLayer?.endPoint = CGPoint
            (x: 1.0, y: 0.5)
        } else {
            gradientLayer?.startPoint = CGPoint
            (x: 0.5, y: 0.0)
            gradientLayer?.endPoint = CGPoint
            (x: 0.5, y: 1.0)
        }
    }
}

var gradientLayer: CAGradientLayer? = nil

override func layoutSubviews() {
    super.layoutSubviews()

    if gradientLayer == nil {
        gradientLayer = CAGradientLayer()
```

```
        gradientLayer!.colors = [
            startColor.cgColor,
            endColor.cgColor
        ]

        if direction == Direction.horizontal.rawValue {
            gradientLayer!.startPoint = CGPoint
            (x: 0.0, y: 0.5)
            gradientLayer!.endPoint = CGPoint
            (x: 1.0, y: 0.5)
        } else {
            gradientLayer!.startPoint = CGPoint
            (x: 0.5, y: 0.0)
            gradientLayer!.endPoint = CGPoint
            (x: 0.5, y: 1.0)
        }

        layer.addSublayer(gradientLayer!)
    }

    gradientLayer?.cornerRadius = layer.cornerRadius
    gradientLayer?.frame = self.bounds
    }
}
```

The GradientView class supports horizontal and vertical gradients only but you can modify it by adding diagonal gradients or even custom angles. A little math in setting the startPoint and endPoint of the gradientLayer will do the trick.

Blurs

The last popular effect, which is particularly popular in iOS, is blur. Blur is a smoothing filter making the whole screen or some part of it... blurry. The effect is so popular that you'll hardly find an iOS user who wouldn't be familiar with it. iPhone and iPad UIs get blurred when you open the notification bar, widget panel, task manager or any other panel on the iOS Home Screen or Lock Screen.

UIKit has a class UIVisualEffectView which can apply blur effect to all underlying views with hardware acceleration. Recipe 4-29 uses it with minimum changes. As we need to apply blur effect not to the view itself, but to views behind it, we need a clear background. By default it's not clear and it can be confusing.

Recipe 4-29. Blurs

```
class BlurView: UIVisualEffectView {
    override init(effect: UIVisualEffect?) {
        super.init(effect: effect)

        commonInit()
    }

    required init?(coder: NSCoder) {
        super.init(coder: coder)

        effect = UIBlurEffect(style: .dark)
        commonInit()
    }

    private func commonInit() {
        backgroundColor = .clear
    }
}
```

The `BlurView` class creates a blur effect and automatically clears the background so it's ready to use. Add `UIView` in the storyboard editor, change the class name to `BlurView` and set the desired blur type – that's it!

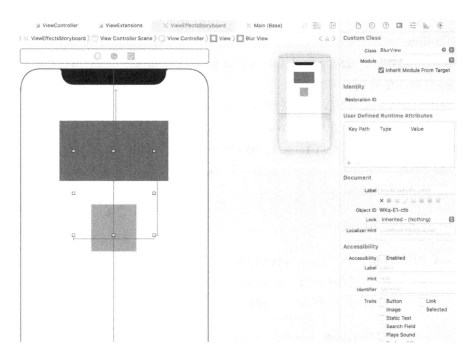

Figure 4-10. Using BlurView in the storyboard

The power of these classes and extensions is that you can use them together. Add a blurry panel with rounded corners, border or even shadow and you'll see how your UI starts to look professional and appealing.

Figure 4-11 shows how three UIViews shown in Figures 4-8, 4-9, and 4-10 look in a running iOS app. This example doesn't use a single line of code, only design in the storyboard.

Figure 4-11. *Custom UIViews in a running iOS app*

Summary

UIKit is a powerful toolkit for developing UI in iOS apps. It appeared in early versions of iOS and actively used up to present day. Still, UIKit often requires a lot of code to do simple things. In this chapter we simplified iOS app navigation, wrote functions to show alerts with just one line of code, reviewed different map options and GPS navigation, The main way to design UI in iOS app is Storyboards. Many features are not available there even being parts of UIKit. Fortunately, it can be easily fixed. Last several recipes show how to add to Storyboards blurs, rounded corners and other effects. In the next chapter we'll talk about another important part of UI development – images.

CHAPTER 5

Image Processing

Showing images on device screens, making them semitransparent, moving them, rotating and scaling them – these are standard features of UIKit. They can be done by showing `UIImage` inside `UIImageView`. But it's not everything you can get on iOS. Apple provides great frameworks to draw and process images. Apart from standard frameworks, there are open source image processing libraries.

What can we do with images? First, we'll learn to load images from files and save them. Files can be stored in the device filesystem, in memory, or even on the Web. Then we'll talk about image downloading and caching and see how libraries like Kingfisher work.

Second, we'll do very simple image processing without using external libraries. They include resizing and cropping. This can be useful for profile pictures. Most apps require them to have a square shape, possibly rounded up to a circle. We already know how to show images with rounded corners, but cropping them to a square before uploading is completely a different topic.

Then we'll discuss image masks. You can show an image with rounded corners by just modifying `UIImageView`'s layer, but in some cases, we need more complex shapes. You may want to allow the user to put an item on top of the picture, like glasses or a beard.

The last topic will be effects and filters. Changing brightness and contrast, gamma, and saturation – all these can be done using external libraries. And even more, popular Instagram-like filters can be applied right in your app. This includes sepia, blur, high/low pass, pixilation, sketch, vignette, swirl, and dozens of other filters.

© Alexander Nekrasov 2022
A. Nekrasov, *Swift Recipes for iOS Developers*,
https://doi.org/10.1007/978-1-4842-8098-0_5

Reading and Writing Images

There are different frameworks when it comes to working with images in iOS. The first one is UIKit. It has class `UIImage`. It's a high-level class giving access to a limited functionality; at the same time it's optimized for working with `UIImageView` and other UIKit components.

`CIImage` from the CoreImage framework is underlying data in `UIImage`. It doesn't provide any functionality for developers, and it's not supposed to be touched directly.

The low-level class is `CGImage`, part of the Core Graphics framework. This class gives full access to image buffer and its characteristics. If you need to change several pixels in an image or apply some filter, `CGImage` is just what you need.

`UIImage`, `CGImage`, and `CIImage` can be converted to each other.

Image Buffer

No matter which class you use, it has a pointer to image buffer – publicly or privately inside its implementation. Image buffer is an array of pixels. Each pixel is encoded by one or several bytes. The most common ways of storing image data are RGB and RGBA. The RBG format uses 3 bytes for each pixel, each byte represents one of these components: red, green, and blue. RGBA uses 4 bytes for each pixel. Besides red, green, and blue, there's also the alpha component indicating how transparent each pixel is (Figure 5-1).

Pixel				Pixel				Pixel				Pixel				Pixel			
R	B	G	A	R	G	B	A	R	G	B	A	R	G	B	A	R	G	B	A
R	B	G	A	R	G	B	A	R	G	B	A	R	G	B	A	R	G	B	A
R	B	G	A	R	G	B	A	R	G	B	A	R	G	B	A	R	G	B	A
R	B	G	A	R	G	B	A	R	G	B	A	R	G	B	A	R	G	B	A
R	B	G	A	R	G	B	A	R	G	B	A	R	G	B	A	R	G	B	A
R	B	G	A	R	G	B	A	R	G	B	A	R	G	B	A	R	G	B	A

Figure 5-1. *Structure of a picture with RGBA palette*

If an image is grayscale, each pixel is usually encoded with 1 byte. If a byte contains 0, it's black; if 255 – white. All values in the middle are different shades of gray.

The class which exposes the most information about image buffer is CGImage. It has the following properties:

- width and height contain image size.

- bitsPerComponent contains the number of bits for a single component.

- bitsPerPixel contains the number of bits per one pixel.

- Other properties.

To draw a picture on a device screen, you need to pass it to a video chip. It understands either pixel buffers in one of the formats mentioned before or in specially prepared textures. In the case of UIKit, you don't need to do it directly. Instead, you just pass it to UIImageView, and it does the rest.

File Formats

Images are stored in files differently than in memory. The most like the pixel buffer image format is BMP (Windows Device Independent Bitmap), but it's rarely used because of its file size. Storing each pixel individually, giving it 3 or 4 bytes of memory, is very consuming. For example, iPhone 11 has a resolution of 828 × 1792 pixels. Even without alpha channel (and BMP doesn't support alpha channel), such a picture needs about 4.24 Mb. An 11-inch iPad Pro's resolution is even higher – 2388 × 1668 pixels. A simple screenshot saved in BMP will take almost 11.4 Mb of device memory. It's suitable for actively used textures, but storing all graphical assets in this format is impossible.

The most popular formats for both iOS app resources and web images are PNG (Portable Network Graphics), JPEG/JPG (Joint Photographic Experts Group), and GIF (Graphics Interchange Format). These formats can be parsed into `UIImage` or `CGImage`. Another compatible format is TIF/TIFF (Tagged Image File Format).

PNG files have good quality and support transparency. At the same time, they're much smaller than BMP or image buffers. PNG is a recommended format for app assets, at least for partially transparent pictures.

The smallest files are encoded with JPG. Depending on the compression rate, they can be smaller with worse quality or larger with better quality. JPG splits the picture into squares and allows only a certain range of colors in each of them. Better quality requires more bytes per each square but gives bigger range. Better compression does the opposite. JPG quality has range from 0 to 1 or from 0 to 10.

GIF pictures are indexed. Instead of color components, GIF uses a color index. Each picture can have up to 256 different colors, which are stored in a palette. Colors outside the palette are not allowed in GIF. Another well-known feature of GIF is animations. GIF may have multiple pictures in one file. A sequence of pictures makes an animation. GIF animations are popular in messengers and in some apps. We'll discuss them in the end of this chapter.

Loading (Reading) Images from Files

After having discussed the ways images are stored both in files and in memory, let's see how to load an image and get an `UIImage` or `CGImage` object.

Image files can be stored in memory, on a disk (flash memory in case of iPhones), or on the Web. Depending on the file location, we'll use different initializers of `UIImage` and `CGImage`.

The first case is when an image file is stored in memory, specifically, in a `Data` object.

Function `loadImageFromData(_:, into:)` decodes a data file passed as a first argument and sets image property of `UIImageView` from the second argument. If the provided file contains a valid image file, the function returns `true`, otherwise `false` (Recipe 5-1).

Recipe 5-1. Loading Images from Memory

```swift
public func loadImageFromData(_ data: Data, into imageView:
UIImageView) -> Bool {
    if let image = UIImage(data: data) {
        imageView.image = image
        return true
    } else {
        return false
    }
}
```

If an app uses downloadable resources, you'll need to open an image from a file (Recipe 5-2), possibly from an archive, but we'll leave it behind the scope.

There are three possible results of this function:

- File not found.

- File is not an image.

- Image was successfully loaded.

Recipe 5-2. Loading Image from Files

```swift
public enum LoadImageError: Error {
    case fileNotFound
    case notAnImage
}
```

```
public func loadImageFromFileWithError(_ file: String, into
imageView: UIImageView) throws {
    guard let data = try? Data(contentsOf: URL(fileURLWithPath:
    file)) else {
        throw LoadImageError.fileNotFound
    }

    if !loadImageFromData(data, into: imageView) {
        throw LoadImageError.notAnImage
    }
}
```

The last possibility is loading a picture directly from the Web. And this way is a little more complicated than it seems to be, first of all, because of caching. Loading images from the Web without at least short-term caching is a user experience disaster. Imagine a user seeing how all the pictures get reloaded when they leave and enter the screen again. And what if the pictures are used in UITableView or UICollectionView?

A simple solution is using an external library. One of them is Kingfisher. It's an extremely popular open source library and free of charge.

If you don't like third-party libraries, you can make a simple caching system right inside your app. We'll discuss it later in this chapter.

Saving (Writing) Images to Files

When the user takes a photo and we process it, we need to save it into one of the popular formats we have mentioned earlier. We can't send it to the server instead of to UIImage, CGImage, or image buffer.

The process is very similar to reading, but we also need to add some arguments – for example, compression rate for JPG format (see Recipe 5-3).

Recipe 5-3. Saving Images to Memory

```swift
func saveImageAsPNG(image: UIImage) -> Data? {
    return image.pngData()
}

func saveImageAsJPEG(image: UIImage, compressionQuality:
CGFloat) -> Data? {
    return image.jpegData(compressionQuality:
    compressionQuality)
}
```

Functions from Recipe 5-4 are not supposed to be used in the project as they increase the amount of code. But they illustrate how converting UIImage to Data is easy.

Saving images to files can be useful as well, for caching purposes or to make a backup copy before processing. Some libraries also require a URL of the file instead of a Data object.

Recipe 5-4. Saving Images to Files

```swift
public enum SaveImageError: Error {
    case dataNotAvailable
}

func saveImageAsPNGFile(image: UIImage, fileName: String)
throws {
    if let data = image.pngData() {
        try data.write(to: URL(fileURLWithPath: fileName))
    } else {
        throw SaveImageError.dataNotAvailable
    }
}
```

```
func saveImageAsJPEGFile(image: UIImage, compressionQuality:
CGFloat, fileName: String) throws {
    if let data = image.jpegData(compressionQuality:
    compressionQuality) {
        try data.write(to: URL(fileURLWithPath: fileName))
    } else {
        throw SaveImageError.dataNotAvailable
    }
}
```

Both functions can throw an exception, so they need to be wrapped into do-try-catch block.

Downloading and Caching Images

We don't usually need to do the downloading and caching of images manually, but it's important to understand the principles. We have an image URL and a cache storage. The storage is basically a `Dictionary`. Keys are URLs, or for better performance, they can be URL hashes. Values are either images or image paths in the local filesystem.

Let's start with the algorithm:

- We get the URL and check if it's in cache.

- If it's in cache, we return the existing image.

- If it's not in cache, we download it and add it to cache.

- Before adding the image to cache, we need to check the cache size. If it has too many elements, we need to clean some of the old data. If the cache contains references to the local filesystem, we can have more items. If all the images are stored in memory, we'd better limit it to 10–20 elements.

Downloading Files

We will review two ways of downloading files. One is using native iOS frameworks – another is with the help of a very popular framework: Alamofire.

File, or specifically image downloading, is no different from any GET request. We compose a request from the URL, headers, arguments, and other data. Depending on the HTTP framework, it can be done differently, but the idea behind it is the same.

As we discuss image processing in this chapter, we'll simplify network components to a minimum. We'll assume that the image is openly located on the Web and doesn't require authorization for downloading.

Downloading Files with Alamofire

Before using Alamofire, you should add it to your project. If you use Swift Package Manager, add this package: `https://github.com/Alamofire/Alamofire`.

For CocoaPods, add this line to your Podfile:

```
pod 'Alamofire'
```

Having the file URL, you can download it with an asynchronous request (see Recipe 5-5). *Asynchronous* means that method call doesn't do all its functionality instantly. Some of it (in our case, downloading) takes time, and this method doesn't hold the app execution until the file is downloaded.

> **Note**   Swift 5.5 offers async/await keywords, making the asynchronous method calls act almost like they're synchronous, removing closures and twisted code. This technology is new, and most of the frameworks don't support it natively, but it's rather easy to turn any function with completion handler into asynchronous function. We'll review it later in this chapter.

Recipe 5-5. Downloading Data with Alamofire

```swift
import Alamofire

func downloadFile(url: String, delegate: @escaping (_ data:
Data?, _ error: Error?) -> Void) {
    AF.request(url)
        .responseData { response in
            DispatchQueue.main.async {
                if let data = response.data {
                    // We have Data object here
                    delegate(data, nil)
                } else {
                    delegate(nil, response.error)
                }
            }
        }
}
```

Downloading Files with URLSession/URLRequest

Using external libraries simplifies the code, but it makes your app heavier in the process. If you're writing a big app, you may want to download files natively as shown in Recipe 5-6 to keep the app as small and fast as possible.

Recipe 5-6. Downloading Files Natively

```swift
func downloadFileNatively(url: URL, delegate: @escaping (_
data: Data?, _ error: Error?) -> Void) {
    let sessionConfig = URLSessionConfiguration.default
    let session = URLSession(configuration: sessionConfig)
    let request = URLRequest(url: url)

    let task = session.dataTask(with: request) { data,
    response, error in
        DispatchQueue.main.async {
            if let data = data {
                // We have Data object here
                delegate(data, nil)
            } else {
                delegate(nil, error)
            }
        }
    }

    task.resume()
}
```

Having a Data object, we can move on to the next step.

Turning Function with Completion Handler into an Asynchronous One

Multiple asynchronous calls make app logic twisted and potentially buggy. When you make an API call, then process it and make more calls depending on the result of the first one, you get either many small functions or one big and nonmaintainable.

In Swift 5.5, Apple introduced a new technology – asynchronous functions. If you work with other programming languages, like JavaScript or Dart, you may already know the concept.

Regular function with completion handler does some work in the background thread and then returns the result into an escaping function passed as an argument. This function usually takes two arguments – correct result and error. For example:

```
func download(url: URL, completion: @escaping (_ result: Data?,
_ error: Error?) -> Void)
```

If downloading is successful, the result Data object is returned, and error is nil. Otherwise, result is nil, and error indicates the problem.

In Swift 5.5, you can rewrite it this way:

```
func downloadAsync(url: URL) async throws -> Data
```

Having the original function with completion handler, we can write the second one as shown in Recipe 5-7.

Recipe 5-7. Async Wrapper

```
func downloadAsync(url: URL) async throws -> Data {
    try await withUnsafeThrowingContinuation { continuation in
        download(url: url) { data, error in
            if let error = error {
                continuation.resume(throwing: error)
            } else if let data = data {
                continuation.resume(returning: data)
            }
            fatalError("Error in download function")
        }
    }
}
```

Replace download with downloadFile or downloadFileNatively, and you'll get an async version of any of these functions. This is how to use it:

```
do {
    let downloadResult = try await downloadAsync(url: url)
    // downloadedResult has a Data object, non-optional
} catch {
    print(error)
}
```

Caching Files in Memory

The simplest and fastest way is to keep downloaded files in memory. The disadvantage is that the memory of iOS apps is rather limited. Even though the limit is high (an app can take up to 5 GB), using a lot of memory is not recommended. iOS may close background apps while your app is in the foreground, and even worse, as soon as your app goes to the background, it will be likely unloaded together with your cache.

Recipt 5-8 shows the simplest implementation of cache without size control.

Recipe 5-8. Simple Memory Cache

```
public class SimpleImageCache {
    private var cache: [Int: Data] = [:]

    public func addToCache(url: String, data: Data) {
        cache[url.hash] = data
    }

    public func getFromCache(url: String) -> Data? {
        cache[url.hash]
    }

    public static let sharedInstance = SimpleImageCache()
}
```

Recipe 5-9 uses this class to implement image loading with cache.

Recipe 5-9. Downloading Files with Cache

```swift
func downloadFileWithCache(url: URL, delegate: @escaping
(_ data: Data?, _ error: Error?) -> Void) {
    if let data = SimpleImageCache.sharedInstance.
    getFromCache(url: url.absoluteString) {
        delegate(data, nil)
        return
    }
    let sessionConfig = URLSessionConfiguration.default
    let session = URLSession(configuration: sessionConfig)
    let request = URLRequest(url: url)

    let task = session.dataTask(with: request) { data,
    response, error in
        if let data = data {
            SimpleImageCache.sharedInstance.addToCache(url:
            url.absoluteString, data: data)
            delegate(data, nil)
        } else {
            delegate(nil, error ?? NSError())
        }
    }

    task.resume()
}
```

When writing asynchronous functions with delegates, we should always remember that all parts of the code should call delegate. Otherwise, the user may get blocked with an eternal loading. It's better to show an error, even if it doesn't have any useful information other than to block the user and force them to close your app (probably forever).

Caching Files in Filesystem

There are two big differences between caching files in memory and in filesystem:

- The memory gets cleaned every time the app is restarted, so we don't need to clean the cache ourselves.

- Cached files aren't stored in a structure like `Dictionary`; we must take care of them ourselves.

The rest is similar.

Obtaining Directory Paths

Before writing any file, we should get a location. There are three possible locations for cache:

- Documents directory
- Caches directory
- Temporary directory

We're not forced to use caches directory to store our cache, but it's a good practice. In different situations, iOS will treat these locations differently. For example, if the phone memory is full, we expect iOS to clean caches and temporary directories. Documents directories of installed apps, on the other hand, shouldn't be touched without the user's direct instruction. Recipe 5-10 shows how to obtain the most common paths.

Recipe 5-10. Obtaining Directory Paths

```
// Get user's documents directory path
func getDocumentDirectoryPath() -> URL {
    let arrayPaths = FileManager.default.urls(for:
    .documentDirectory, in: .userDomainMask)
```

```
    let docDirectoryPath = arrayPaths[0]
    return docDirectoryPath
}

// Get user's cache directory path
func getCacheDirectoryPath() -> URL {
    let arrayPaths = FileManager.default.urls(for:
    .cachesDirectory, in: .userDomainMask)
    let cacheDirectoryPath = arrayPaths[0]
    return cacheDirectoryPath
}

// Get user's temp directory path
func getTempDirectoryPath() -> URL {
    let tempDirectoryPath = URL(fileURLWithPath:
    NSTemporaryDirectory(), isDirectory: true)
    return tempDirectoryPath
}
```

Saving Files to Cache

Now when we decided that we store our cache in a folder created specifically for this purpose, and we have its path in a URL object, we can save downloaded files and retrieve them as needed.

Apart from the files themselves, we need to store extra data about them – for example, the original URL. As we'll see soon enough, having the last use date and size would be also useful for the next step.

We need to have a known URL as well as the local file name. An obvious solution would be to give the files names that match their URL. Obvious, but wrong. The problem is that file names have restrictions in both length and allowed characters. The good news is that we don't need a full URL; we only need the hash. We can use a hash instead of a URL.

In Recipe 5-11, we'll modify the `SimpleImageCache` class and turn it into `FileImageCache`.

Recipe 5-11. File Image Cache

```
public class SimpleFileImageCache {
    private func getCacheDirectoryPath() -> URL {
        let arrayPaths = FileManager.default.urls(for:
        .cachesDirectory, in: .userDomainMask)
        let cacheDirectoryPath = arrayPaths[0]
        return cacheDirectoryPath
    }

    private func getLocalURL(url: String) -> URL {
        let baseURL = getCacheDirectoryPath()
        return baseURL.appendingPathComponent("\(url.hash)")
    }

    public func addToCache(url: String, data: Data) {
        let localURL = getLocalURL(url: url)
        _ = try? data.write(to: localURL, options: .atomic)
    }

    public func getFromCache(url: String) -> Data? {
        let localURL = getLocalURL(url: url)
        return try? Data(contentsOf: localURL)
    }

    public static let sharedInstance = SimpleFileImageCache()
}
```

The `getCacheDirectoryPath` function is turned into a private method, but it can be used from our previous recipe directly.

The addToCachemethod doesn't always succeed. For example, if the memory is full, it will fail. But this shouldn't completely break the app; it will just make it glitchy. It's not good, but there's not much to do to handle this situation. We don't even need to show error popups. With many failed attempts, it can break the app much worse.

Verifying Cache Size

Depending on the storage place, there are two different ways to verify the cache size:

- If the cached files are stored in memory, we can go through all Data objects and sum up their sizes.

- If the cached files are stored in filesystem, we need either to calculate all sizes or store them in an indexing file.

Now when we're having cleaner cache, we'll need to store date and time to remove the oldest ones. And here's the question: Do we need to delete the files that were downloaded earlier, or the ones that were used earlier? Both solutions are valid, but the second one is more effective. Recipe 5-12 offers a new ImageCache class based on previous solutions to keep the data of the last use and update it every time the image is accessed. When the cache is full, we'll delete 30% of the images, which are out of use longer than others.

Enough words, back to coding!

Recipe 5-12. Memory Caching System

```
public class ImageCache {
    private struct CachedFile {
        var hash: Int
        var size: Int {
```

```
            data.count
        }
        var data: Data
        var lastAccess: Date
    }

    private var cache: [Int: CachedFile] = [:]
    var totalSize: Int {
        var size = 0
        for f in cache.values {
            size += f.size
        }
        return size
    }

    var sizeThreshold = 104_857_600 // 100Mb

    public func addToCache(url: String, data: Data) {
        var totalSize = self.totalSize
        if totalSize + data.count > sizeThreshold {
            // Remove 10% of cached files
            let sortedFiles = cache.values.sorted { cf1, cf2 in
                cf1.lastAccess.timeIntervalSince1970 < cf2.
                lastAccess.timeIntervalSince1970
            }
            while totalSize + data.count > sizeThreshold *
            9 / 10 {
                guard let lastFile = sortedFiles.last else {
                    break
                }

                totalSize -= lastFile.size
                cache.removeValue(forKey: lastFile.hash)
            }
```

```
        }

        cache[url.hash] = CachedFile(hash: url.hash, data:
        data, lastAccess: Date())
    }

    public func getFromCache(url: String) -> Data? {
        guard var cacheFile = cache[url.hash] else {
            return nil
        }

        cacheFile.lastAccess = Date()
        return cacheFile.data
    }

    public static let sharedInstance = ImageCache()
}
```

The CachedFile structure contains all necessary information about the cached file. The lastAccess field is modified every time the image is requested.

The sizeThreshold field defines how much memory can be used for cache. By default, it's 100 megabytes. The addToCache method checks if the new image fits, and if it doesn't, it removes files until the cache has at least 10% free memory after adding a new file.

The next version of our caching system (Recipe 5-13), FileImageCache, has the same principle behind. It creates cache in init and cleans 10% in deinit, if necessary.

Recipe 5-13. Filesystem Caching System

```
public class FileImageCache {
    private struct CachedFile {
        var hash: Int
        var size: Int
```

```
    var lastAccess: Date
}

private var cache: [Int: CachedFile] = [:]
var totalSize: Int {
    var size = 0
    for f in cache.values {
        size += f.size
    }
    return size
}

private func getCacheDirectoryPath() -> URL {
    let arrayPaths = FileManager.default.urls(for:
    .cachesDirectory, in: .userDomainMask)
    let cacheDirectoryPath = arrayPaths[0]
    if !FileManager.default.fileExists(atPath:
    cacheDirectoryPath.path) {
        do {
            try FileManager.default.createDirectory(at:
            cacheDirectoryPath, withIntermediateDirectories:
            true, attributes: nil)
        } catch {
            print(error)
        }
    }
    return cacheDirectoryPath
}

private func getLocalURL(url: String) -> URL {
    let baseURL = getCacheDirectoryPath()
    return baseURL.appendingPathComponent("\(url.hash)")
}
```

```
init() {
    // Get a list of files from filesystem
    do {
        let fileURLs = try FileManager.default.
        contentsOfDirectory(at: getCacheDirectoryPath(),
        includingPropertiesForKeys: nil, options:
        [.skipsHiddenFiles, .skipsSubdirectoryDescendants])
        for fileURL in fileURLs {
            guard let hash = Int(fileURL.
            lastPathComponent) else {
                continue
            }

            let attributes = try? FileManager.default.
            attributesOfItem(atPath: fileURL.path)
            let fileSize = attributes?[.size] as?
            UInt64 ?? 0

            cache[hash] = CachedFile(hash: hash, size:
            Int(fileSize), lastAccess: Date())
        }
    } catch {
        print("Error loadign cache from filesystem")
    }
}

deinit {
    cleanIfNeeded()
}

var sizeThreshold = 104_857_600 // 100Mb

private func cleanIfNeeded(newFileSize: Int = 0) {
```

```swift
    var totalSize = self.totalSize
    if totalSize + newFileSize > sizeThreshold {
        // Remove 10% of cached files
        let sortedFiles = cache.values.sorted { cf1, cf2 in
            cf1.lastAccess.timeIntervalSince1970 < cf2.
            lastAccess.timeIntervalSince1970
        }
        while totalSize + newFileSize > sizeThreshold *
        9 / 10 {
            guard let lastFile = sortedFiles.last else {
                break
            }

            do {
                try FileManager.default.removeItem(atPath:
                getLocalURL(url: "\(lastFile.hash)").
                absoluteString)
                totalSize -= lastFile.size
            } catch {
                print(error.localizedDescription)
            }
            cache.removeValue(forKey: lastFile.hash)
        }
    }
}

public func addToCache(url: String, data: Data) {
    cleanIfNeeded(newFileSize: data.count)

    do {
        try data.write(to: getLocalURL(url: url))
```

```swift
            cache[url.hash] = CachedFile(hash: url.hash, size:
            data.count, lastAccess: Date())
        } catch {
            print(error.localizedDescription)
        }
    }

    public func getFromCache(url: String) -> Data? {
        guard var cacheFile = cache[url.hash] else {
            return nil
        }

        cacheFile.lastAccess = Date()

        let fullURL = getLocalURL(url: url)

        do {
            return try Data(contentsOf: fullURL)
        } catch {
            print(error)
            return nil
        }
    }

    public static let sharedInstance = FileImageCache()
}
```

These two methods can be joined into one. Memory cache can have a small amount of data, for example, 10–15 Mb. Filesystem cache – several times more. When memory cache reaches its limit, it saves some files on the disk and then retrieves them when necessary.

How could it be useful? Imagine that you're writing an app showing a restaurant menu. It has UITableView or UICollectionView with small pictures. The user scrolls up and down trying to decide what they're in the mood to eat this day. This is a good situation for memory cache. It will take longer to read files from the disk again and again, even if this disk is a high-speed flash memory. Then the user goes to their cart, and we no longer need menu pictures, so we can remove them from the memory. On the other hand, they can go back to the menu or browse it after ordering. We simply load all the pictures back from the disk.

We'll leave two-level cache out of scope in this book, but you can try to make your own as an exercise. It would be a valuable experience.

To wrap it up, let's review a usage example. We'll put three UIKit views to the screen:

```
// UILabel showing current cache size
@IBOutlet weak var lblCacheSize: UILabel!

// UITextField to enter URL
@IBOutlet weak var tfURL: UITextField!

// UIImageView to show loaded (or cached) image
@IBOutlet weak var ivImage: UIImageView!
```

Plus, we add two buttons. One will load an image using memory cache; another will use filesystem cache. They'll trigger the following actions:

```
@IBAction func loadUsingMemory()
@IBAction func loadUsingFiles()
```

Storyboard design may look like Figure 5-2.

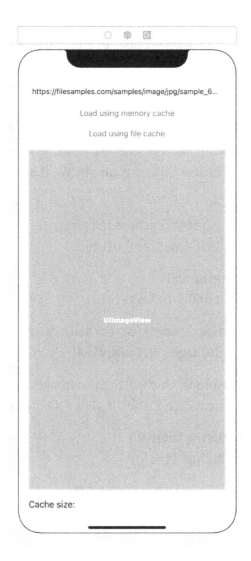

Figure 5-2. *Storyboard of image cache view*

To better understand this, let's now review an image cache usage example.

The example is straightforward; let's just make several clarifications:

1. Some functions accept URL; others require `String`. If we're talking about files, URL starts with `file://`, so to convert it to a file path, we need `.path` instead of `.absoluteString`.

2. To create a URL object from a text string entered inside text field `tfURLString`, we need to escape characters; otherwise, the URL can be nil. For this purpose, we use the `.addingPercentEncod ing(withAllowedCharacters: CharacterSet. urlQueryAllowed)` method.

3. Empty spaces can also *break* URL, so we need to trim entered `String`: `.trimmingCharacters(in: .whitespacesAndNewlines)`.

Resizing and Cropping

Having access to image buffer in `CGImage`, we can modify it – either inside an existing image object or by creating a new image buffer and turning it into a new `CGImage` or `UIImage`.

What can we do with an image?

*   Scale it. Proportionally or not. Upscale or downscale it.

*   Crop it. We can crop an image to a square or rectangle of the proportions we need. The cropped image will be always smaller than the original one.

Image Scaling

There are two types of scaling: upscaling and downscaling. In the first case, the new image is bigger than the original one; in the second case – smaller. If scaling is not proportional, it can be both upscaling and downscaling. But we usually need to preserve the aspect ratio, so we won't investigate this case here.

Fortunately, the CoreImage framework does everything for us; we only need to calculate the new size. What can it be?

We may need to set the maximum size of an image, for example, if the user chooses a profile picture. Modern iPhone cameras have very high resolution. Image sizes around 5000 × 5000 pixels are normal. But it's not necessary for profile pictures, so the app needs to downscale it.

If the user chooses a picture from the gallery, it can be too small. In this case, we need to upscale it. Alternatively, the app can show an alert asking to choose a better-quality picture. Recipe 5-14 shows a possible resizing solution, while Recipe 5-15 only downscales the image.

Recipe 5-14. Scaling an Image to the Required Size

```
extension UIImage {
    func resized(maxSize: CGFloat) -> UIImage? {
        let scale: CGFloat
        if size.width > size.height {
            scale = maxSize / size.width
        }
        else {
            scale = maxSize / size.height
        }

        let newWidth = size.width * scale
        let newHeight = size.height * scale
```

```
        UIGraphicsBeginImageContext(CGSize(width: newWidth,
        height: newHeight))
        draw(in: CGRect(x: 0, y: 0, width: newWidth, height:
        newHeight))
        let newImage = UIGraphicsGetImageFromCurrentImageContext()
        UIGraphicsEndImageContext()
        return newImage
    }
}
```

Recipe 5-15. Downscaling an Image

```
extension UIImage {
    func downscaled(maxSize: CGFloat) -> UIImage? {
        let maxDimension = size.width > size.height ? size.
        width : size.height
        if maxDimension > maxSize {
            return resized(maxSize: maxSize)
        } else {
            return self
        }
    }
}
```

Now it's time to discuss *Image Context*. Changing pixels in UIImage or CGImage is not efficient. If we calculate pixels manually, we lose all graphic acceleration. The right way to do it is to create an Image Context.

You can work with one Image Context at a time. All work takes place between:

```
UIGraphicsBeginImageContext
// ... and ...
UIGraphicsEndImageContext
```

You can use the `UIImage` instances to draw in the current context, or you can draw lines or other shapes using `UIBezierPath` and other classes using Image Context.

In the end, you need to turn the context into a new `UIImage` object using the `UIGraphicsGetImageFromCurrentImageContext` function.

Image Cropping

This is required when we need a specific aspect ratio. Many apps require square pictures. For example, all posts on Instagram are square. Profile pictures are usually square as well. Sometimes rounded, sometimes circular. From an image processing point of view, squares, rounded squares, and circles are the same, because rounding is performed by UIKit, and the difference is only in the corner radius.

Another option is a rectangle. Computer displays often have a 16:9 ratio. Full HD is 1920 × 1080. If you divide 1920 by 16 or 1080 by 9, you get 120. UHD or 4K has twice more pixels in each dimension – 3840 × 2160. If you divide width by 16 or height by 9, the result is 240 in both cases.

iPad screens have an aspect ratio of 4:3. For example, a typical iPad Pro screen with retina has a resolution of 2048 × 1536 pixels. 512 × 4 = 2048, 512 × 3 = 1536. iPad Pro's aspect ratio is not a perfect 4:3, but it's rather close. For example, an 11-inch iPad Pro has a resolution of 2388 × 1668 pixels. It's 1.43:1, or 4.29:3.

When writing an app, it's more important to keep the necessary aspect ratio rather than the resolution. There are several ways to change the aspect ratio:

- Scaling an image without preserving the aspect ratio. It's the easiest way, but the result will be stretched.

- Cropping an image. If the original image is too wide, we can remove some pixels from its sides.

- Adding padding. When you watch movies at home, you can see that most of them have a black space on the top and bottom of the screen. That's because at the cinema the aspect ratio is different (the screen is wider), and movies are usually optimized for cinema.

Let's write two extensions of UIImage. The one from Recipe 5-16 will crop it to a square using the smallest dimension. Another, from Recipe 5-17, will crop it to the required aspect ratio.

Recipe 5-16. Cropping an Image to a Square

```swift
extension UIImage {
    var squared: UIImage? {
        guard let originalCGImage = self.cgImage else {
            return nil
        }

        // Create a copy of the image without the
        imageOrientation property so it is in its native
        orientation
        let contextImage: UIImage = UIImage(cgImage:
        originalCGImage)

        // Get the size of the contextImage
        let contextSize: CGSize = contextImage.size

        let posX: CGFloat
        let posY: CGFloat
        let width: CGFloat
        let height: CGFloat

        // Check to see which length is the longest and create
        the offset based on that length, then set the width and
        height of our rect
        if contextSize.width > contextSize.height {
```

```
            posX = (contextSize.width - contextSize.height) / 2
            posY = 0
            width = contextSize.height
            height = contextSize.height
        } else {
            posX = 0
            posY = (contextSize.height - contextSize.width) / 2
            width = contextSize.width
            height = contextSize.width
        }

        let rect: CGRect = CGRect(x: posX, y: posY, width:
        width, height: height)

        if let imageRef = contextImage.cgImage?.
        cropping(to: rect) {
            // Create a new image based on the imageRef and
            rotate back to the original orientation
            return UIImage(cgImage: imageRef, scale: self.
            scale, orientation: self.imageOrientation)
        } else {
            return nil
        }
    }
}
```

Recipe 5-17. Cropping an Image to a Custom Aspect Ratio

```
extension UIImage {
    func changeAspectRatio(aspectRatio: CGFloat) -> UIImage? {
        guard let originalCGImage = self.cgImage else {
            return nil
        }
```

```
// Create a copy of the image without the
imageOrientation property so it is in its native
orientation
let contextImage: UIImage = UIImage(cgImage:
originalCGImage)

// Get the size of the contextImage
let contextSize: CGSize = contextImage.size

let posX: CGFloat
let posY: CGFloat
let width: CGFloat
let height: CGFloat

if aspectRatio == contextSize.width / contextSize.
height {
    // New aspect ratio is the same as old
    posX = 0
    posY = 0
    width = contextSize.width
    height = contextSize.height
} else if aspectRatio < contextSize.width /
contextSize.height {
    // New aspect ratio is less then original
    // Cut from left/right
    posX = (contextSize.width - contextSize.height *
    aspectRatio) / 2
    posY = 0
    width = contextSize.height * aspectRatio
    height = contextSize.height
} else {
    // Cut from top/bottom
    posX = 0
```

```
            posY = (contextSize.height - contextSize.width /
            aspectRatio) / 2
            width = contextSize.width
            height = contextSize.width / aspectRatio
        }

        let rect: CGRect = CGRect(x: posX, y: posY, width:
        width, height: height)

        // Create bitmap image from context using the rect
        if let imageRef = contextImage.cgImage?.
        cropping(to: rect) {
            return UIImage(cgImage: imageRef, scale: self.
            scale, orientation: self.imageOrientation)
        } else {
            return nil
        }
    }
}
```

Note   These computed property and function should always succeed, but if something can go wrong, we assume it will. That's why the result is optional. What could be wrong exactly? For example, the aspect ratio can be so small or so big that one of the dimensions will be zero; or the device can run out of memory – in these cases, we may really get nil.

Preparing and Showing Profile Pictures

We can't control the geometry of the photos the user takes. If we pull said photos from social networks, we have even less control. There's always the option to show an error if the user tries to download a picture of wrong size or wrong aspect ratio, but it will create a bad user experience.

A better solution is to process the picture before uploading. We usually want to limit the picture size and make it square. Let's say, in our example, we'll limit it to 512 × 512 pixels.

Processing Profile Pictures Before Uploading

Having previously written extensions, we can prepare profile picture in just one like of code as shown in Recipe 5-18. Here's our algorithm:

- The user takes a picture. The source doesn't matter; it can be a camera or gallery.

- If both width and height are bigger than 512 pixels, we downscale it, so at least one of the dimensions will be 512 pixels (the other one will be bigger).

- If the width is not equal to the height, we crop the image. To make it simple, we'll cut pixels equally from both sides.

Recipe 5-18. Processing an Image to Upload As Profile Picture

```
extension UIImage {
    func prepareProfilePicture() -> UIImage {
        squared?.downscaled(maxSize: 512) ?? self
    }
}
```

As you can see, this is a combination of previously written functions. We can return an optional `UIImage` if one of them fails. An alternative option is to return the original image as in the preceding recipe.

Showing Profile Pictures

If the profile picture is properly prepared, we can be sure that it's going to be a square, each dimension not bigger than 512 pixels. On the other hand, mistakes happen. Fortunately, `UIImageView` can show any picture as a square, a rounded square, or even a circle, depending on the design needed (see Figure 5-3 and Recipe 5-19).

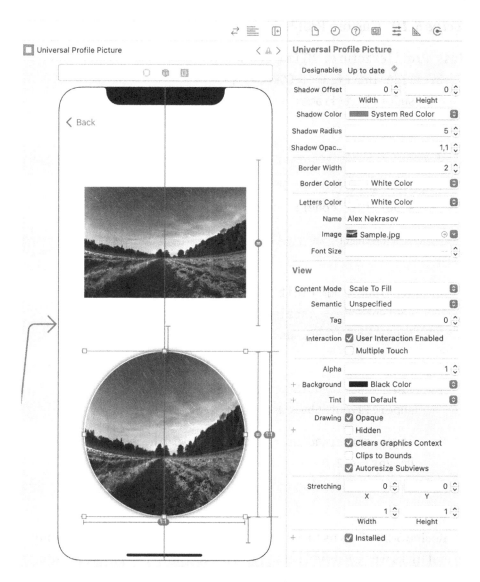

Figure 5-3. *Universal profile picture view*

Recipe 5-19. Custom Profile Pictures View

```swift
class ProfilePicture: UIImageView {
    override init(frame: CGRect) {
        super.init(frame: frame)

        commonInit()
    }

    required init?(coder: NSCoder) {
        super.init(coder: coder)

        commonInit()
    }

    private func commonInit() {
        contentMode = .scaleAspectFill
        layer.masksToBounds = true
    }

    override func layoutSubviews() {
        super.layoutSubviews()

        layer.cornerRadius = min(bounds.width, bounds.
        height) / 2.0
    }
}
```

Recipe 5-20 offers us to enhance the app look with effects. Combining several tricks we've learned before, let's make a universal profile picture component with a shadow, outline, and the user's initials if the picture is not uploaded.

Recipe 5-20. Universal Profile Picture Component

```swift
@IBDesignable
class UniversalProfilePicture: UIView {
    @IBInspectable var shadowOffset: CGSize {
        get {
            layer.shadowOffset
        }

        set {
            layer.shadowOffset = newValue
        }
    }

    @IBInspectable var shadowColor: UIColor? {
        get {
            if let sc = layer.shadowColor {
                return UIColor(cgColor: sc)
            } else {
                return nil
            }
        }

        set {
            layer.shadowColor = newValue?.cgColor
        }
    }

    @IBInspectable var shadowRadius: CGFloat {
        get {
            layer.shadowRadius
        }

        set {
```

```
            layer.shadowRadius = newValue
        }
    }

    @IBInspectable var shadowOpacity: Float {
        get {
            layer.shadowOpacity
        }

        set {
            layer.shadowOpacity = newValue
        }
    }

    @IBInspectable var borderWidth: CGFloat = 2.0 {
        didSet {
            layer.borderWidth = borderWidth
        }
    }

    @IBInspectable var borderColor: UIColor = .white {
        didSet {
            layer.borderColor = borderColor.cgColor
        }
    }

    @IBInspectable var lettersColor: UIColor = .white {
        didSet {
            self.setInitials()
        }
    }

    @IBInspectable var name: String = "John Doe" {
        didSet {
```

```
        self.setInitials()
    }
}

@IBInspectable var image: UIImage? {
    didSet {
        picture?.image = image
    }
}

@IBInspectable var fontSize: CGFloat = 32 {
    didSet {
        self.setInitials()
    }
}

var picture: UIImageView?
var initials: UILabel?

override init(frame: CGRect) {
    super.init(frame: frame)

    commonInit()
}

required init?(coder: NSCoder) {
    super.init(coder: coder)

    commonInit()
}

private func commonInit() {
    picture = UIImageView(frame: bounds)
    initials = UILabel(frame: bounds)

    addSubview(initials!)
```

```
        addSubview(picture!)

        picture?.contentMode = .scaleToFill
        picture?.layer.masksToBounds = true
        picture?.image = image
        initials?.textAlignment = .center

        setInitials()
    }

    override func layoutSubviews() {
        super.layoutSubviews()

        picture?.frame = bounds
        initials?.frame = bounds

        layer.cornerRadius = min(bounds.width, bounds.
        height) / 2.0
        picture?.layer.cornerRadius = min(bounds.width, bounds.
        height) / 2.0
        initials?.layer.cornerRadius = min(bounds.width,
        bounds.height) / 2.0
    }

    private func setInitials() {
        initials?.font = UIFont.systemFont(ofSize: fontSize)
        let initialsText = name
            .components(separatedBy: " ")
            .reduce("") {
                ($0 == "" ? "" : "\($0.first!)") + "\($1.first!)"
            }
        initials?.text = initialsText
        initials?.textColor = lettersColor
    }
}
```

The last recipe copies some of the functionality described earlier. Using the UIView extensions from Chapter 3, the UniversalProfilePicture class can be smaller.

Image Masks

The previous sections of this chapter explained how to do basic image processing. The next step is to combine two or more pictures into one. All popular messengers, social networks, blogging platforms, and other apps offer to add effects that don't change the image itself but add something on top of it. It can be text, a simple drawing, a sticker, smoke, stars, etc.

This can be done by adding an image with transparency on top of another. The top image can be one of the predefined images, an image selected by the user or a newly generated one.

The key concept here is alpha channel. Images consist of pixels. Each pixel has channels representing either one of the colors or level of transparency. The most common palette on computer devices, including smartphones, is RGBA. RGBA stands for red, green, blue, and alpha.

Red, green, and blue are color components. The mixture of these colors gives the whole display palette. Red and green make yellow; red and blue make magenta; blue and green make cyan. When all channels are at their maximum value, it's white.

The alpha component is a level of transparency. If it takes 1 byte, its range is from 0 to 255, where 0 means a fully transparent pixel and 255 is a fully opaque pixel.

But why is all this important?

Merging Images

When we merge images into one, we merge each channel separately using alpha as a multiplier. Assuming that the background image is not transparent, we can merge them this way:

```
r = (r1 * (255 - a2) + r2 * a2) / 255
g = (g1 * (255 - a2) + g2 * a2) / 255
b = (b1 * (255 - a2) + b2 * a2) / 255
```

Or if the colors are represented as Float or Double values, we can merge them like this:

```
r = r1 * (1.0 - a2) + r2 * a2
g = g1 * (1.0 - a2) + g2 * a2
b = b1 * (1.0 - a2) + b2 * a2
```

These formulas can be nonlinear, but this is the simplest solution, and it demonstrates how the alpha channel is used.

In Recipe 5-21, we have two images. The first image can be fully opaque. The second one is partially transparent, and its size is the same as that of the first image or smaller.

Recipe 5-21. Merging Two Images – Simple Case

```
extension UIImage {
    func simpleMerge(with topImage: UIImage, x: CGFloat, y:
    CGFloat) -> UIImage? {
        UIGraphicsBeginImageContext(CGSize(width: size.width,
        height: size.height))
        draw(at: CGPoint(x: 0, y: 0))
        topImage.draw(at: CGPoint(x: x, y: y))
        let newImage =
        UIGraphicsGetImageFromCurrentImageContext()
```

```
        UIGraphicsEndImageContext()
        return newImage
    }
}
```

Let's take it to the next level (Recipe 5-22). Now, we'll assume that images can have any size; the resulting image will contain both source images without cropping.

Recipe 5-22. Merging Two Images – Universal Case

```
extension UIImage {
    func universalMerge(with topImage: UIImage, x: CGFloat, y:
    CGFloat) -> UIImage? {
        let x1 = (x < 0) ? -x : 0
        let y1 = (y < 0) ? -y : 0
        let x2 = (x < 0) ? 0 : x
        let y2 = (y < 0) ? 0 : y

        let newWidth = max(x1 + size.width, x2 + topImage.
        size.width)
        let newHeight = max(y1 + size.height, y2 + topImage.
        size.height)

        UIGraphicsBeginImageContext(CGSize(width: newWidth,
        height: newHeight))
        draw(at: CGPoint(x: x1, y: y1))
        topImage.draw(at: CGPoint(x: x2, y: y2))
        let newImage =
        UIGraphicsGetImageFromCurrentImageContext()
        UIGraphicsEndImageContext()
        return newImage
    }
}
```

Sometimes we need to keep the original size and make the resulting image the same as the background one. In this case we ignore the pixels of the second image which are outside the background picture as shown in Recipe 5-23.

Recipe 5-23. Merging Two Images with Cropping

```
extension UIImage {
    func croppingMerge(with topImage: UIImage, x: CGFloat, y:
    CGFloat) -> UIImage? {
        let cropX = (x < 0) ? -x : 0
        let cropY = (y < 0) ? -y : 0
        let cropW: CGFloat
        let cropH: CGFloat
        if x < 0 {
            cropW = min(topImage.size.width + x, size.width)
        } else {
            cropW = min(topImage.size.width, size.width -
            x - cropX)
        }
        if y < 0 {
            cropH = min(topImage.size.height + y, size.height)
        } else {
            cropH = min(topImage.size.height, size.height -
            y - cropY)
        }
        if cropW <= 0 || cropH <= 0 {
            return self
        }

        let topImageCropped: UIImage
        if cropW == topImage.size.width && cropH == topImage.
        size.height {
```

```
        topImageCropped = topImage
    } else {
        guard let topCGImage = topImage.cgImage,
            let imageRef = topCGImage.cropping(to: CGRect(x:
            cropX, y: cropY, width: cropW, height: cropH))
        else {
            return nil
        }

        topImageCropped = UIImage(cgImage: imageRef)
    }
    UIGraphicsBeginImageContext(CGSize(width: size.width,
    height: size.height))
    draw(at: CGPoint(x: 0, y: 0))
    topImageCropped.draw(at: CGPoint(x: max(x, 0), y:
    max(y, 0)))
    let newImage =
    UIGraphicsGetImageFromCurrentImageContext()
    UIGraphicsEndImageContext()
    return newImage
    }
}
```

Note   If you tested these recipes, you probably noticed that simple merge and merge with cropping give the same result. It happens because the UIImage draw method crops the image if part of it is out of bounds. Basically, Recipe 5-23 shows what happens under the hood. It's totally valid to use any of these options.

Applying Mask

If you have a rectangular image, for example, one from an iPhone camera, and you want to give it some other shape, you may need to apply a mask. A mask is an image containing only one channel – alpha. As using alpha as the only channel is not allowed in any image format, usually grayscale images are used as masks.

The white color represents fully opaque pixels, while black represents fully transparent ones. Let's say that m is a level of whiteness of a mask pixel.

```
a = a1 * m // If m has a range from 0.0 to 1.0
// or
a = a1 * m / 255 // If m has a range from 0 to 255
```

Red, green, and blue channels stay untouched when we apply a mask.

In Recipe 5-24, we will apply a mask. If the mask is smaller than the original image, we'll assume that the pixels outside the mask are transparent. If the mask partially goes beyond the image bounds, we'll ignore those pixels.

Unlike previous recipes, in this one, we'll work directly with image buffer.

Recipe 5-24. Applying a Mask to an Image

```
extension UIImage {
    func apply(mask: UIImage) -> UIImage? {
        guard let originalCGImage = cgImage,
            let maskCGImage = mask.cgImage
        else {
            return nil
        }

        let colorSpace = CGColorSpaceCreateDeviceRGB()
        let bytesPerPixel = 4
```

```
let bytesPerRow = bytesPerPixel * originalCGImage.width
let bytesPerRowMask = bytesPerPixel * maskCGImage.width
let bitsPerComponent = 8
let bitmapInfo: UInt32 = CGImageAlphaInfo.
premultipliedLast.rawValue

guard let context = CGContext(data: nil, width:
originalCGImage.width, height: originalCGImage.height,
bitsPerComponent: bitsPerComponent, bytesPerRow:
bytesPerRow, space: colorSpace, bitmapInfo:
bitmapInfo),
    let ptr = context.data?.assumingMemoryBound(to:
    UInt8.self) else {
  return nil
}

guard let contextMask = CGContext(data: nil, width:
maskCGImage.width, height: maskCGImage.height,
bitsPerComponent: bitsPerComponent, bytesPerRow:
bytesPerRowMask, space: colorSpace, bitmapInfo:
bitmapInfo),
    let ptrMask = contextMask.data?.
    assumingMemoryBound(to: UInt8.self) else {
  return nil
}

context.draw(originalCGImage, in: CGRect(x: 0, y: 0,
width: originalCGImage.width, height: originalCGImage.
height))
contextMask.draw(maskCGImage, in: CGRect(x: 0, y: 0,
width: maskCGImage.width, height: maskCGImage.height))

for y in 0..<originalCGImage.height {
    let lineOffset = y * bytesPerRow
```

```
            let maskLineOffset = y * bytesPerRowMask
            for x in 0..<originalCGImage.width {
                let pixelOffset = lineOffset + (x *
                bytesPerPixel)
                let maskPixelOffset = maskLineOffset + (x *
                bytesPerPixel)
                if x >= maskCGImage.width || y >= maskCGImage.
                height {
                    ptr[pixelOffset + 3] = 0
                } else {
                    ptr[pixelOffset + 3] = UInt8((U
                    Int(ptrMask[maskPixelOffset]) +
                    UInt(ptrMask[maskPixelOffset + 1]) +
                    UInt(ptrMask[maskPixelOffset])) / 3)
                }
                ptr[pixelOffset] = UInt8(UInt(ptr[pixelOffset])
                * UInt(ptr[pixelOffset + 3]) / 255)
                ptr[pixelOffset + 1] =
                UInt8(UInt(ptr[pixelOffset + 1]) *
                UInt(ptr[pixelOffset + 3]) / 255)
                ptr[pixelOffset + 2] =
                UInt8(UInt(ptr[pixelOffset + 2]) *
                UInt(ptr[pixelOffset + 3]) / 255)
            }
        }

        guard let resultCGImage = context.makeImage() else {
            return nil
        }
        return UIImage(cgImage: resultCGImage)
    }
}
```

This may look complicated if you never worked with image buffers directly as it's not common practice for programmers. But if you're writing an app or a game using image processing, this can be very useful.

Let's review it in details. First, we need to get nonoptional references to CGImage objects.

```
guard let originalCGImage = cgImage,
      let maskCGImage = mask.cgImage
else {
    return nil
}
```

Then we define parameters for the images. We need them to create context. Even if the original images don't have an alpha-channel, the new image should.

```
let colorSpace = CGColorSpaceCreateDeviceRGB()
let bytesPerPixel = 4
let bytesPerRow = bytesPerPixel * originalCGImage.width
let bytesPerRowMask = bytesPerPixel * maskCGImage.width
let bitsPerComponent = 8
let bitmapInfo: UInt32 = CGImageAlphaInfo.premultipliedLast.
rawValue
```

The most complicated part is *premultiplied alpha*. What is it? In an image with premultiplied alpha or a *premultiplied image*, all components of each pixel are multiplied by the alpha value of the same pixel. This is the way video acceleration works.

Note   Nontransparent pixels have the same values as pixels without
alpha-channel, from 0 to 255. Fully transparent pixels will have 0 in
all four components.

The next step is to create context and raw pointers for both image
and mask.

```
guard let context = CGContext(data: nil, width:
originalCGImage.width, height: originalCGImage.height,
bitsPerComponent: bitsPerComponent, bytesPerRow: bytesPerRow,
space: colorSpace, bitmapInfo: bitmapInfo),
    let ptr = context.data?.assumingMemoryBound(to: UInt8.
    self) else {
  return nil
}

guard let contextMask = CGContext(data: nil, width:
maskCGImage.width, height: maskCGImage.height,
bitsPerComponent: bitsPerComponent, bytesPerRow:
bytesPerRowMask, space: colorSpace, bitmapInfo: bitmapInfo),
    let ptrMask = contextMask.data?.assumingMemoryBound(to:
    UInt8.self) else {
  return nil
}
```

Types of both `ptr` and `ptrMask` are `UnsafeMutablePointer<UInt8>`.
If you worked with the C language family (including Objective-C), it's the
same as `unsigned char *`. It can be indexed the same way as an array.

As both contexts were initialized with `nil`, we need to draw the original
image and mask on these contexts:

```
context.draw(originalCGImage, in: CGRect(x: 0, y: 0, width:
originalCGImage.width, height: originalCGImage.height))
contextMask.draw(maskCGImage, in: CGRect(x: 0, y: 0, width:
maskCGImage.width, height: maskCGImage.height))
```

Then pixel by pixel, we apply the mask:

```
for y in 0..<originalCGImage.height {
    let lineOffset = y * bytesPerRow
    let maskLineOffset = y * bytesPerRowMask
    for x in 0..<originalCGImage.width {
        let pixelOffset = lineOffset + (x * bytesPerPixel)
        let maskPixelOffset = maskLineOffset + (x *
        bytesPerPixel)
        if x >= maskCGImage.width || y >= maskCGImage.height {
            ptr[pixelOffset + 3] = 0
        } else {
            ptr[pixelOffset + 3] = UInt8((UInt(ptrMask[maskPix
            elOffset]) + UInt(ptrMask[maskPixelOffset + 1]) +
            UInt(ptrMask[maskPixelOffset])) / 3)
        }
        ptr[pixelOffset] = UInt8(UInt(ptr[pixelOffset]) *
        UInt(ptr[pixelOffset + 3]) / 255)
        ptr[pixelOffset + 1] = UInt8(UInt(ptr[pixelOffset + 1])
        * UInt(ptr[pixelOffset + 3]) / 255)
        ptr[pixelOffset + 2] = UInt8(UInt(ptr[pixelOffset + 2])
        * UInt(ptr[pixelOffset + 3]) / 255)
    }
}
```

The constants lineOffset and maskLineOffset indicate the start
pointer of each line. We can calculate it for each pixel, but it's faster to save
them for each line.

Multiple conversions to UInt and UInt8 are an essential part of the calculation. We can't safely add two UInt8 variables without a risk of overflow. Before assigning it back to ptr, we need to convert the result back to UInt8. Of course, after calculation, it should be in the range from 0 to 255.

This algorithm is not the most optimized. This is just a generic solution. Having a particular task, it's possible to optimize it as needed.

Effects and Filters

It's possible to apply filters working directly with pixel buffer or with Image Context, but it's not the most efficient way. Modern iOS devices have good GPUs, which are optimized to do image processing.

CoreImage

Apple offers the CoreImage framework, which has hardware-accelerated filters for images. Recipe 5-25 shows how to apply a Gaussian blur to the UIImage object:

Recipe 5-25. Gaussian Blur with CoreImage

```
import CoreImage

extension UIImage {
    func gaussianBlur(radius: CGFloat) -> UIImage? {
        let ciContext = CIContext(options: nil)

        guard let blurFilter = CIFilter(name:
        "CIGaussianBlur") else {
            return nil
        }
```

```
blurFilter.setValue(CIImage(image: self), forKey:
"inputImage")
blurFilter.setValue(radius, forKey: "inputRadius")

guard let outputImageData = blurFilter.value(forKey:
"outputImage") as? CIImage,
    let outputImage = ciContext.
    createCGImage(outputImageData, from:
    outputImageData.extent)
else {
    return nil
}

return UIImage(cgImage: outputImage)
    }
}
```

The problem of this framework is the lack of good protocols. Instead of predefined constants, methods, and classes, it uses String arguments for the filter type and arguments.

GPUImage

The GPUImage framework is an open-source library available on GitHub. The first generation of this framework was written in Objective-C back in 2013. More modern versions are GPUImage2 and GPUImage3. They have similar interfaces; the difference is in the version of Swift.

To add it, use one of the repositories on Brad Larson's GitHub account: https://github.com/BradLarson. Repositories on this account have all the necessary documentation.

Note   GPUImage2 and GPUImage3 are not available via CocoaPods.
You can use the Swift Package Manager instead.

Using GPUImage, you can get comfortable shortcuts for the CoreImage
features, plus additional filters and effects. Recipe 5-26 shows how to apply
the same Gaussian blur with GPUImage:

Recipe 5-26. Gaussian Blur with GPUImage

```
import GPUImage

extension UIImage {
    func gaussianBlurGPU(radius: CGFloat) -> UIImage? {
        let blurFilter = GPUImageGaussianBlurFilter()
        blurFilter.blurRadiusInPixels = radius

        return blurFilter.image(byFilteringImage: self)
    }
}
```

GIF Animations

Animated GIFs appeared in 1987, but now they're popular as never before.
But they have two serious restrictions:

- They have indexed colors. Each GIF file has a palette
  containing up to 256 colors. It can use the same color
  twice or more, but it can't use more colors in the same
  picture.

- GIFs don't support semitransparent pixels. If you show
  a GIF picture or animation over another picture, it will
  have a sharp edge.

GIFs are good for small animations, not for clips or movies.

iOS doesn't show GIF animations out of the box. You need to write some code or use a library that will do it for you.

AnimatedImageView from Kingfisher

Kingfisher is a popular framework for downloading images from the Internet. It has an integrated caching system; it offers real-time image processing and ready-to-use views.

To add Kingfisher using the Swift Package Manager, add the following link: `https://github.com/onevcat/Kingfisher`

There's also a pod for this. If you prefer CocoaPods, add this line:

```
pod 'Kingfisher'
```

One of those views is `AnimatedImageView`. It's a subclass of `UIImageView`, which makes it easy to use. You can use it both locally and remove GIF files inside `AnimatedImageView`. Recipe 5-27 shows how to create it programmatically and play online GIFs in a loop.

Recipe 5-27. Using AnimatedImageView

```
import Kingfisher

func createAndPlayAnimatedImageView(parentView: UIView, gifURL:
URL, delegate: AnimatedImageViewDelegate?) {
    let animatedImageView = AnimatedImageView(frame:
    parentView.bounds)
    animatedImageView.delegate = delegate

    animatedImageView.kf.setImage(with: gifURL, placeholder:
    nil, options: nil) { result in
        switch result {
        case .success:
```

```
            animatedImageView.startAnimating()

        case .failure(let error):
            print(error.localizedDescription)
        }
    }

    parentView.addSubview(animatedImageView)
}
```

Note   If you use this code in a production environment, don't forget about possible layout changes.

SwiftyGif

SwiftyGif is a framework created specifically for playing GIF animations. Its biggest advantage is that it works inside a standard `UIImageView`. It supports both local and remote GIF files.

To add SwiftyGif to your project using Swift Package Manager, add the following link: `https://github.com/kirualex/SwiftyGif`.

To add it with CocoaPods, modify your Podfile:

```
pod 'SwiftyGif'
```

Recipes 5-28 and 5-29 show how we can repeat the previous recipe, but using SwiftyGif instead of Kingfisher.

Recipe 5-28. Loading Remote GIF with SwiftyGif

```
import SwiftyGif

func createAndPlaySwiftyGif(parentView: UIView, gifURL: URL,
delegate: SwiftyGifDelegate?) {
```

```
let imageview = UIImageView(gifURL: gifURL, manager:
.defaultManager, loopCount: -1)
imageview.frame = parentView.bounds
imageview.delegate = delegate
parentView.addSubview(imageview)
}
```

Another advantage of SwiftyGif is the ability to load animations from an app bundle.

Recipe 5-29. Loading GIFs from an App Bundle

```
import SwiftyGif

func loadLocalGif(name: String, into imageView: UIImageView) {
    if let gifImage = try? UIImage(gifName: name) {
        imageView.setGifImage(gifImage)
    }
}
```

When loaded, the animation can be controlled by UIImageView methods:

```
imageView.startAnimatingGif()
imageView.stopAnimatingGif()
imageView.showFrameAtIndexDelta(delta: Int)
imageView.showFrameAtIndex(index: Int)
```

Summary

Images present in all iOS apps, one way or another. Sometimes it's as simple as showing bundled images, sometimes they require loading and processing. In this chapter we talked about different representations of images, in UIKit, in memory and in file system. We discussed loading images from web, with using external libraries and without, paying attention at caching as a part of this mechanism. We upscaled and downscaled images to get desired size, changed geometry and processed existing images. We reviewed simple effects like Gaussian blur. Finally, we looked at more complex case of showing images – showing animations. In the next chapter we'll continue talking about UIKit, particularly, text editing.

CHAPTER 6

Text Editing

Another important aspect of iOS development is text editing. On mobile platforms, adding text inputs is particularly difficult because of several complications:

- The on-screen keyboard appears when you enter UITextField. It can hide other UI elements or even the text field itself.

- The on-screen keyboard doesn't disappear itself. In some cases, it can follow you to another screen.

- The on-screen keyboard has different heights on different devices. Even if you know the sizes for all existing models, new iPhones or iPads will eventually appear, and the keyboard height on them may be different.

- A physical keyboard can be connected to an iOS device. Besides special keyboards for iPads, any Bluetooth keyboard can be connected to said devices. When a physical keyboard is connected, the on-screen keyboard doesn't appear.

- Even setting the keyboard type doesn't guarantee that the user won't type a *forbidden* symbol.

© Alexander Nekrasov 2022
A. Nekrasov, *Swift Recipes for iOS Developers*,
https://doi.org/10.1007/978-1-4842-8098-0_6

Besides these mobile-specific problems, we have common problems of all apps allowing user input:

- We may need to format the text in a specific way, for example, phone number or credit card number.

- We often need floating text, which follows your input. Or prefix. It's especially popular when you need input for money. It may require both formatting and floating text with currency.

We will discuss all these problems and their solutions in this chapter. And as a bonus, we'll create a pin pad, a UI component containing four text inputs for four digits.

Ready? Open Xcode. Go!

Analyzing User Input in Real Time

Many beginner developers don't understand how to process text input in real time. There's a `UITextFieldDelegate` delegate protocol containing many useful functions, but nothing like `whatUserJustTyped` or `afterThisInputTextWillBeLikeThis`.

Why would we need it? After all, we can always catch the moment when the user ends editing or accesses the text property of `UITextField` as they tap some button. Even though that's true, modern applications are not like web forms from the 1990s – they're interactive, and they follow your actions and adjust the UI accordingly. Here are several examples:

- If you can log in with a phone number or an email address, the text input can change its formatting when it understands what you're entering exactly. The app can also change some texts and icons around.

- When the user enters a bank card number, it's a good practice to show the logo of the card system (Visa, MasterCard, or other) after entering the first couple of digits. Some apps even show the logo of the issuing bank. When you use an app like that, you feel much more confident, and you feel that you're on the right path.

- When the user fills in a form and makes a mistake, apps often highlight the problematic fields. The app should remove warnings or errors when the user starts typing.

- When the user enters a correct phone number, bank account number, taxpayer number, or any other data of the sort that can be verified, some apps show a success icon and/or move focus to the next field.

- Pin pad. We'll discuss it later, but a pin pad requires real-time input processing.

The key function for us is this:

```
optional func textField(_ textField: UITextField,
shouldChangeCharactersIn range: NSRange,
      replacementString string: String) -> Bool
```

It looks complicated, but this callback is extremely powerful. It provides us with all the necessary information:

- textField is a UITextField object (or a subclass of UITextField) where editing occurred.

- range shows a range of symbols *removed* from text input. If it has zero length, it's just a position of insertion.

- string contains new characters. It can be one
  character if the user tapped a key on the on-screen
  keyboard, or a whole text string if the user pasted it
  from the clipboard.

Method returns a Boolean value. If you return true, "replacement" (or insertion) will occur; otherwise, the input will be blocked.

Two components are missing:

- Text before change

- Text after change

Text before change is simply textField.text. *Text after change* requires some kind of *calculation (Recipe 6-1).*

Recipe 6-1. Getting Text After Change

```
extension ViewController: UITextFieldDelegate {
    func textField(_ textField: UITextField,
    shouldChangeCharactersIn range: NSRange, replacementString
    string: String) -> Bool {
        if let text = textField.text,
            let textRange = Range(range, in: text) {
             let updatedText = text.replacingCharacters(in:
             textRange, with: string)
             // UpdatedText contains text after input is
                processed
        }
        return true
    }
}
```

Please note that you must be very careful with the return value of this method. For example, if you return *true* only if validation passes, the user won't be able to enter even the first symbol.

Usually, the code inside this delegate function should handle three situations:

- The entered text is not valid and shouldn't be entered at all.

- The entered text is valid, but the result is not valid.

- Everything is valid; we can show the user that they did well.

False should be returned in the first situation only, for example, when the user enters a phone number, and the string argument has a letter or emoji.

The second important note – *always* allow backspace or any other deletion method. If by mistake an *illegal* character appears in your text field, the user should be able to remove it. So if the string argument is empty, it should never return false.

Now let's make a simple validator in Recipe 6-2. All validators are different, but the basic structure is similar. Let's say we need the user's email address. Our EmailInputValidator class should be assigned as a delegate of UITextField. It will remove all the characters that are not allowed in email addresses and make a call to its own delegate function when an address is valid.

Please find String extension isValidEmail in Recipe 3-3 or in full version of Recipe 6-2 on GitHub.

Recipe 6-2. Email Input Validator

```
protocol EmailInputValidatorDelegate: AnyObject {
    func validityChanged(isValid: Bool)
}

class EmailInputValidator: NSObject, UITextFieldDelegate {
    weak var delegate: EmailInputValidatorDelegate?
```

259

```
    func textField(_ textField: UITextField,
    shouldChangeCharactersIn range: NSRange, replacementString
    string: String) -> Bool {
        let allowedRegEx = "[A-Z0-9a-z._%+-@]+"
        let allowedTest = NSPredicate(format: "SELF MATCHES
        %@", allowedRegEx)
        if !allowedTest.evaluate(with: string) && !string.
        isEmpty {
            return false
        }

        if let text = textField.text,
           let textRange = Range(range, in: text) {
            let updatedText = text.replacingCharacters(in:
            textRange, with: string)
            delegate?.validityChanged(isValid: updatedText.
            isValidEmail)
        }
        return true
    }
}
```

You can use it in UIViewController like this:

```
class ViewController: UIViewController {
    @IBOutlet weak var textField: UITextField!

    var emailValidator = EmailInputValidator()

    override func viewDidLoad() {
        super.viewDidLoad()
        textField.delegate = emailValidator
        emailValidator.delegate = self
    }
}
```

```
extension ViewController: EmailInputValidatorDelegate {
    func validityChanged(isValid: Bool) {
        print(isValid)
    }
}
```

Formatting User Input

There's a certain type of data that needs visual decoration to be understandable, for example, phone numbers. They have different lengths in different countries, but on average, they're around ten digits long. Seeing ten digits without any separation is hard for humans – you'll hardly recognize your own phone number if presented that way. Adding some spaces, brackets, and dashes makes a phone number much more readable and understandable.

Another example is bank card numbers. It also varies, but the most common is separating digits in blocks by four.

We can't expect perfect text styling from users. Even more, we usually allow to type only digits in such fields – on-screen keyboards don't have spaces, dashes, or brackets. We need to do it automatically.

Formatting Phone Numbers

The next recipe will use the libPhoneNumber library. You can add it from the following repository: https://github.com/iziz/libPhoneNumber--iOS. If you use Swift Package Manager, type the URL there; otherwise, use pod:

```
pod 'libPhoneNumber-iOS'
```

Recipe 6-3. Formatting Phone Numbers in UITextField

```swift
import libPhoneNumber_iOS

class PhoneViewController: UIViewController, UITextFieldDelegate {
    @IBOutlet weak var phoneNumberTextField: UITextField!

    let countryId = "US"

    let phoneUtil = NBPhoneNumberUtil.sharedInstance()

    func textField(_ textField: UITextField,
    shouldChangeCharactersIn range: NSRange, replacementString
    string: String) -> Bool {
        if string.isEmpty {
            return true
        }
        if let text = textField.text,
            let textRange = Range(range, in: text) {
             let updatedText = text.replacingCharacters(in:
             textRange, with: string)
             if let phoneUtil = self.phoneUtil,
                let phoneNumber = try? phoneUtil.
                parse(updatedText, defaultRegion: countryId),
                let formattedString = try? phoneUtil.
                format(phoneNumber, numberFormat: .NATIONAL) {
                 DispatchQueue.main.async {
                     textField.text = formattedString
                 }
            }
        }
        return true
    }
}
```

Let's review it line by line.

In your UI file (storyboard or xib), add a country selector and a UITextField. The country selector is usually a list of flags, country names, or codes. Changing country should change the countryId variable. We'll leave this behind our scope. UITextField should have an @IBOutlet and View Controller as a delegate.

We create a constant phoneUtil as a reference to an NBPhoneNumberUtil singleton.

All the logic is inside a delegate method. If the string is empty, we return true without any verifications. It will allow us to freely delete symbols even if the result is not a valid phone number. Letting users delete symbols from UITextField is very important for a friendly UI.

```
if string.isEmpty {
    return true
}
```

Then we calculate updatedText the way we discussed before in this chapter.

```
let updatedText = text.replacingCharacters(in: textRange,
with: string)
```

Now, when we have updated the text, we try to parse it and format it as a national number using countryId as a parameter. formattedString either has a formatted number or nil. If it has content, we set it as a new text.

And this part requires our attention as it's very important. We can't set text directly because the change of textField occurs after true is returned. If we change the text property inside this function, it will be overridden. That's why we wrap it into DispatchQueue.main.async.

```
DispatchQueue.main.async {
    textField.text = formattedString
}
```

Formatting Bank Card Numbers

The idea behind credit card number formatting is exactly the same as the one behind phone number formatting, but in this case, we don't need any libraries. Recipe 6-4 shows how it can be achieved.

Recipe 6-4. Formatting Bank Card Numbers in UITextField

```
extension String {
    func group(by groupSize: Int = 4, separator: String = " ")
    -> String {
        if count <= groupSize { return self }

        let splitIndex = index(startIndex, offsetBy: groupSize)

        return String(self[..<splitIndex]) + separator +
            String(self[splitIndex...]).group(by: groupSize,
            separator:separator)
    }
}

class CreditCardViewController: UIViewController,
UITextFieldDelegate {
    @IBOutlet weak var cardNumberTextField: UITextField!

    func textField(_ textField: UITextField,
    shouldChangeCharactersIn range: NSRange, replacementString
    string: String) -> Bool {
        if string.isEmpty {
            return true
        }
        if let text = textField.text,
            let textRange = Range(range, in: text) {
              let updatedText = text
```

```
        .replacingCharacters(in: textRange,
        with: string)
        .filter("0123456789".contains)
    let formattedString = updatedText.group()
        .trimmingCharacters(in: .whitespacesAndNewlines)
    DispatchQueue.main.async {
        textField.text = formattedString
    }
}
return true
}
}
```

In real life, credit card numbers can be more complicated, but we just group digits by four. In more complex cases, we can detect the card type by the first digits and apply proper formatting.

After getting `updatedText`, we leave only digits and drop all other characters (which are spaces). Then we add a space after each four digits and set new text inside the `DispatchQueue.main.async` block.

As a helper function, we use the group extension method of String. It's rather straightforward; it takes first `groupSize` characters of a string, adds a separator, and does the same with the rest of the string recursively. As a result, with default arguments, it groups digits by four and inserts spaces between.

Working with Emojis

Emojis appeared in the 1980s and became popular in the 1990s. Back then, there were no pictures, just text signs. Eyes were a colon; noses, a dash; and mouths – brackets. Like this: :-). You could see a face only by turning your head to the side, but it was better than nothing. Without seeing your interlocutor or hearing their voice, you didn't know their intonation.

Within time, emojis became a big part of Internet culture and little by little migrated to other aspects of our lives. The Unicode Consortium adds more and more emojis to the standard; on-screen keyboards have a separate layout with emojis; finally, they became not just pictures, but often animated pictures.

At the same time, emojis can be a problem for us, developers. Even being standardized, emojis still can be encoded differently, and new emojis may not be supported by old devices or old versions of operating systems. That's why it's better to block them from most text inputs. They can be totally acceptable in social network posts, comments, and video descriptions, but users shouldn't be able to use emojis in fields for email addresses, passwords, legal names, bank account numbers, etc.

To block users from entering emojis, we need two steps:

- Detect that String has emojis.

- Block texts with emojis from the UITextField delegate.

Detecting Emojis in Strings

Similarly to string analyzers from Chapter 3, let's add some extensions to detect if String has emojis (Recipe 6-5). As we know, String is a sequence of Character instances. To make sure String doesn't have emojis, we need to check each Character. To check if String has emojis, we need to find at least one Character, which is an emoji.

Recipe 6-5. Checking If Character Is Emoji

```
extension Character {
    var isSimpleEmoji: Bool {
        guard let firstScalar = unicodeScalars.first else {
        return false }
```

```
        return firstScalar.properties.isEmoji && firstScalar.
        value > 0x238C
    }

    var isCombinedIntoEmoji: Bool { unicodeScalars.count > 1 &&
    unicodeScalars.first?.properties.isEmoji ?? false }

    var isEmoji: Bool { isSimpleEmoji || isCombinedIntoEmoji }
}
```

What's the difference between a simple emoji and a combined one? The problem is that modern emojis are not just faces and flowers, they have many other characteristics like skin tone, hair color, and gender. If a simple yellow face can be represented as one Unicode symbol, more complicated ones are sequences of symbols.

The computed property isEmoji tells if Character is any type of emoji regardless of its complexity. Other extensions from Recipe 6-6 can be used to detect if String contains emojis.

Recipe 6-6. Checking If String Contains Emoji

```
extension String {
    var isSingleEmoji: Bool { count == 1 && containsEmoji }

    var containsEmoji: Bool { contains { $0.isEmoji } }

    var containsOnlyEmoji: Bool { !isEmpty && !contains { !$0.
    isEmoji } }

    var emojiString: String { emojis.map { String($0)
    }.reduce("", +) }

    var emojis: [Character] { filter { $0.isEmoji } }

    var emojiScalars: [UnicodeScalar] { filter { $0.isEmoji
    }.flatMap { $0.unicodeScalars } }
}
```

We don't need all these computer properties to analyze user input, but they can be useful for other purposes. For example, if you ask your user to characterize some post with three emojis, the `containsOnlyEmoji` function will be handy.

Blocking Emoji from User Input

To block emojis from user input, we just need to combine some of our previous recipes. Recipe 6-7 shows what we get.

Recipe 6-7. Blocking Emoji from User Input

```swift
extension ViewController: UITextFieldDelegate {
    func textField(_ textField: UITextField,
    shouldChangeCharactersIn range: NSRange, replacementString
    string: String) -> Bool {
        if string.containsEmoji && !string.isEmpty {
            return false
        }

        // Validate if necessary

        return true
    }
}
```

Floating Prefix or Suffix

Sometimes, we need to add noneditable text strings to the beginning or end of `UITextField`. It can be currency, a validation badge, or any other information.

Depending on the text position (prefix or suffix), there are different methods. To add a prefix, we need to add padding to the text input. Suffixes are more complicated; we need to move them every time the editable text is changed.

Adding Prefix

To add a prefix, you need two steps:

- Add a `UILabel` object and properly align it.

- Add padding to `UITextField`, so the editable text will be to the right of the prefix.

Let's create two objects and add outlets:

```
@IBOutlet weak var prefixLabel: UILabel!
@IBOutlet weak var mainText: TextFieldWithPadding!
```

Note   TextFieldWithPadding is a class created in the "UITextField Paddings" section in Chapter 4. You can find its source code in Recipe 4-26.

We need to know the width of `prefixLabel`. If it's static, we can adjust it in `viewDidLayoutSubviews`. If not, we need to readjust it every time the text is changed.

```
mainText.paddingLeft = prefixLabel.bounds.width + 8
```

We add eight extra points for a gap between the prefix and the main text. The full solution is shown in Recipe 6-8.

Recipe 6-8. UITextField with Prefix

```
class FloatingPrefixViewController: UIViewController {
    @IBOutlet weak var prefixLabel: UILabel!
    @IBOutlet weak var mainText: TextFieldWithPadding!

    static let gapWidth = CGFloat(8)

    override func viewDidLayoutSubviews() {
        mainText.paddingLeft = prefixLabel.bounds.width +
        FloatingPrefixViewController.gapWidth
    }

    func setPrefix(_ prefix: String) {
        prefixLabel.text = prefix
        DispatchQueue.main.async {
            self.mainText.paddingLeft = self.prefixLabel.
            bounds.width + FloatingPrefixViewController.
            gapWidth
        }
    }
}

extension FloatingPrefixViewController: UITextFieldDelegate {
    func textFieldShouldReturn(_ textField: UITextField) -> Bool {
        setPrefix(textField.text ?? "")
        textField.text = ""
        return false
    }
}
```

As you can see, the setPrefix method has an asynchronous part. We need it to let UILabel update before using its new width. If asynchronous parts are not acceptable for you, you can calculate the text width manually.

For demo purposes, this recipe contains an extension setting a new label text every time the user taps *return*. Don't use this extension in a real-life app.

Adding Suffix

Unlike prefixes, suffixes are not static; they move every time you enter a piece of text. Instead of adding padding when the layout is ready, we need to add the UITextField delegate and override func textField(_: UITextField, shouldChangeCharactersIn: NSRange, replacementString: String) -> Bool.

The vertical alignment is the same as in the previous recipe, but horizontally, UILabel should be aligned with the left (leading) side of UITextField. We will change this constraint every time the user changes input.

Another possible problem is the space on the right (trailing) side. If the entered text with a suffix is wider than our area, the label will go beyond the area, or the text will be cropped. That's why we need to use the same class TextFieldWithPadding, but with rightPadding instead of leftPadding. Recipe 6-9 provides a solution for a floating suffix problem.

Recipe 6-9. UITextField with Suffix

```
class FloatingSuffixViewController: UIViewController,
UITextFieldDelegate {
    @IBOutlet weak var suffixLabel: UILabel!
    @IBOutlet weak var mainText: TextFieldWithPadding!
    @IBOutlet weak var suffixLeadingSpace: NSLayoutConstraint!

    static let gapWidth = CGFloat(8)
```

```swift
    override func viewDidLayoutSubviews() {
        mainText.paddingRight = suffixLabel.bounds.width +
        FloatingPrefixViewController.gapWidth
    }

    func setSuffix(_ suffix: String) {
        suffixLabel.text = suffix
        DispatchQueue.main.async {
            self.mainText.paddingLeft = self.suffixLabel.
            bounds.width + FloatingPrefixViewController.
            gapWidth
        }
    }

    func textField(_ textField: UITextField,
    shouldChangeCharactersIn range: NSRange, replacementString
    string: String) -> Bool {
        if let text = textField.text,
            let textRange = Range(range, in: text) {
            let updatedText = text.replacingCharacters(in:
            textRange, with: string)
            if let font = mainText.font {
                let fontAttributes = [NSAttributedString.Key.
                font: font]
                let size = (updatedText as NSString).
                size(withAttributes: fontAttributes)
                suffixLeadingSpace.constant = size.width
                view.layoutIfNeeded()
            }
        }
        return true
    }
}
```

Width calculation here is performed through the NSString method size. It returns a CGSize structure containing text width and height with given attributes. The only attribute we set is NSAttributedString.Key. font. In iOS, the UIFont object contains not only the font but also font size, so the size method has enough information to calculate.

Keyboard Handling

As we discussed in the beginning of this chapter, on-screen keyboards can be a big problem for a developer. By default, the keyboard will appear when the user taps UITextField or UITextView, but it won't disappear itself, and it will do nothing but to overlap UITextField or UITextView. If you add a field in the bottom of the screen, the keyboard will overlap it.

Hiding the Keyboard When the User Clicks the Outside Text Field

If the text field is not inside a scrollable area, it's rather easy to hide it. You only need to override one function in UIViewController and call view. endEditing(true) as shown in Recipe 6-10.

Recipe 6-10. Hiding the Keyboard

```
class HidingKeyboardViewController: UIViewController {
    override func touchesBegan(_ touches: Set<UITouch>, with
    event: UIEvent?) {
        super.touchesBegan(touches, with: event)
        view.endEditing(true)
    }
}
```

Hiding the Keyboard in Scrollable Areas

If you need text input inside a scrollable area, which is rather typical for forms, the previous recipe won't work. It doesn't mean you shouldn't use it; the user can tap the outside scrollable area, but it won't be enough.

There are two solutions depending on your desired behavior:

- Hiding the keyboard when the user scrolls

- Hiding the keyboard when the user taps outside text fields

The first solution requires setting one attribute of `UIScrollView`. In Interface Builder (a storyboard editor), select your `UIScrollView` and set *Keyboard* to *Dismiss on drag*.

You can do the same using code:

```
scrollView.keyboardDismissMode = .onDrag
```

Hiding the Keyboard When the User Leaves the Screen

When the user leaves the screen, it's a good practice to hide the on-screen keyboard. There are usually two directions:

- Moving to the next screen

- Going back to the previous screen

Let's say, you have a Next button with the `@IBAction` function. The first line of code in this function should be

```
view.endEditing(true)
```

As for going back, the solution is similar. In Chapter 4, we created a universal function `goBack`. Recipe 6-11 updates it to hide the keyboard. If the keyboard is not shown, it won't harm the app.

Recipe 6-11. Updated goBack Function

```
public extension UIViewController {
    @IBAction func goBack() {
        view.endEditing(true)
        if let nc = navigationController,
           nc.viewControllers.count >= 2 {
            nc.popViewController(animated: true)
        } else {
            dismiss(animated: true, completion: nil)
        }
    }
}
```

Changing Your Layout When the Keyboard Appears

When the keyboard appears, your layout needs to change. Always. Even if your text fields are always on top of the screen, there are objects in the bottom, which need to be moved. In case of using scrollable areas like UIScrollView, the content offset can be adjusted as well.

This can be done by handling keyboard notifications as shown in Recipe 6-12.

Recipe 6-12. Handling Keyboard Notifications

```
class KeyboardListenerViewController: UIViewController {
    override func viewWillAppear(_ animated: Bool) {
        super.viewWillAppear(animated)

        NotificationCenter.default.addObserver(
            self,
            selector:
            #selector(keyboardWillShow(notification:)),
            name: UIResponder.keyboardWillShowNotification,
```

```
            object: nil
        )
        NotificationCenter.default.addObserver(
            self,
            selector: #selector(keyboardWillHide(notification:)),
            name: UIResponder.keyboardWillHideNotification,
            object: nil
        )
    }

    override func viewDidDisappear(_ animated: Bool) {
        NotificationCenter.default.removeObserver(self, name:
        UIResponder.keyboardWillShowNotification, object: nil)
        NotificationCenter.default.removeObserver(self, name:
        UIResponder.keyboardWillHideNotification, object: nil)

        super.viewWillDisappear(animated)
    }

    @objc func keyboardWillShow(notification: NSNotification) {
        if let keyboardSize = (notification.
        userInfo?[UIResponder.keyboardFrameEndUserInfoKey] as?
        NSValue)?.cgRectValue.size {
            // Keyboard height is in keyboardSize.height
        }
    }

    @objc func keyboardWillHide(notification: NSNotification) {
        // We don't usually need keyboard size when it's
        disappearing, so just set back your constraints
    }
}
```

The notification argument is optional; you can create handlers without it if you don't need keyboard size. Don't forget that if the function signature changes, #selector should reflect these changes.

Now, when we know the moments of keyboard appearance and disappearance, let's adjust our layout. One of the possible solutions is to create a constraint; let's call it bottomConstraint, which defines the distance between the bottom of the screen (or safe area) and the lowest view. Usually, it's the Next button.

From passed notification, we can extract keyboard height and move layout accordingly as shown in Recipe 6-13.

Recipe 6-13. Changing Layout When Keyboard Is Appearing and Disappearing

```
class KeyboardListenerViewController2: UIViewController {
    @IBOutlet weak var bottomConstraint: NSLayoutConstraint!

    override func viewWillAppear(_ animated: Bool) {
        super.viewWillAppear(animated)

        NotificationCenter.default.addObserver(
            self,
            selector: #selector(keyboardWillShow(notification:)),
            name: UIResponder.keyboardWillShowNotification,
            object: nil
        )
        NotificationCenter.default.addObserver(
            self,
            selector: #selector(keyboardWillHide),
            name: UIResponder.keyboardWillHideNotification,
            object: nil
        )
    }
```

```swift
override func viewDidDisappear(_ animated: Bool) {
    NotificationCenter.default.removeObserver(self, name:
    UIResponder.keyboardWillShowNotification, object: nil)
    NotificationCenter.default.removeObserver(self, name:
    UIResponder.keyboardWillHideNotification, object: nil)

    super.viewWillDisappear(animated)
}

@objc func keyboardWillShow(notification: NSNotification) {
    if let keyboardSize = (notification.
    userInfo?[UIResponder.keyboardFrameEndUserInfoKey] as?
    NSValue)?.cgRectValue.size {
        bottomConstraint.constant = keyboardSize.height
        view.layoutIfNeeded()
    }
}

@objc func keyboardWillHide() {
    bottomConstraint.constant = 0
    view.layoutIfNeeded()
}
}
```

Scrolling to Show Current Text Field

When the form is big like shown on Figure 6-1, we use a scrollable area, usually UIScrollView. When the keyboard is shown, we have a rather small area, and after two to three text fields, the cursor goes beyond its bounds. We need to automatically scroll UIScrollView to make the field that is being edited now visible.

There are two ways of handling it. First, you can shrink UIScrollView and make it completely above the keyboard. This way has a big disadvantage – every time the keyboard appears, the size of UIScrollView changes, and it can create unpleasant visual effects. The second way is to change the content offset (scroll position) every time the user enters another UITextField. As we know the position in parent, we know which content offset to set. Recipe 6-14 shows this solution.

Figure 6-1. *Moving UITextFields when the keyboard appears*

Recipe 6-14. Scrolling to Make Text Field Visible

```
class AutoscrollViewController: UIViewController {
    @IBOutlet weak var scrollView: UIScrollView!
    @IBOutlet weak var textField1: UITextField!
    @IBOutlet weak var textField2: UITextField!
    @IBOutlet weak var textField3: UITextField!
    @IBOutlet weak var textField4: UITextField!
    @IBOutlet weak var textField5: UITextField!
    @IBOutlet weak var textField6: UITextField!
    @IBOutlet weak var textField7: UITextField!
    @IBOutlet weak var textField8: UITextField!
    // ...

    static let gap = CGFloat(40)
}

extension AutoscrollViewController: UITextFieldDelegate {
    func textFieldDidBeginEditing(_ textField: UITextField) {
        let offset = textField.frame.origin.y -
        AutoscrollViewController.gap
        DispatchQueue.main.async {
            self.scrollView.setContentOffset(CGPoint(x: 0, y:
            offset), animated: true)
        }
    }

    func textFieldShouldReturn(_ textField: UITextField)
-> Bool {
        switch textField {
        case textField1: textField2.becomeFirstResponder()
        case textField2: textField3.becomeFirstResponder()
        case textField3: textField4.becomeFirstResponder()
```

```
    case textField4: textField5.becomeFirstResponder()
    case textField5: textField6.becomeFirstResponder()
    case textField6: textField7.becomeFirstResponder()
    case textField7: textField8.becomeFirstResponder()
    default: textField.resignFirstResponder()
    }
    return false
  }
}
```

This code also includes a *Return* button handler. When you tap *Return/ Next/Submit* or another button (it is always located in the bottom-right corner, and the name depends on the UITextField configuration), it goes to the next field.

You can invent a more interesting scrolling mechanism, for example, to make the previous field visible, or scroll only when the field is partially or fully covered. But this is a totally working solution, so feel free to use it as is.

Pin Pad UI Component

Passwords are being used less and less, and it makes sense. Most users either forget their passwords or use the same password in all websites and mobile apps, which is extremely unsafe.

Many modern apps offer either a two-step verification with an SMS code or a code from a verification app (like Google Authenticator or Authy). This code contains four to six digits. Sometimes, they replace the password altogether.

The most beautiful and comfortable way to handle this is a *pin pad*. A regular UITextField doesn't look good for this purpose.

Let's write a simple four-digit pin pad.

First, add four UITextField objects to your view as shown in Figure 6-2. You can locate them wherever you like, but it will be better to make center alignment and put them on top, so we won't need to change the layout when the keyboard appears.

Figure 6-2. *Pin pad example*

Choose Number Pad as the keyboard type for all four of them. Assign them tags from 0 to 3 in order.

Make four outlets:

```
@IBOutlet weak var digit1TextField: UITextField!
...
@IBOutlet weak var digit4TextField: UITextField!
```

Make your UIViewController subclass (in our case, it's PinPadViewController) a delegate for all of them. Implement UITextFieldDelegate. We will need these methods:

```
func textFieldShouldBeginEditing(_ textField:
UITextField) -> Bool
func textField(_ textField: UITextField,
shouldChangeCharactersIn range: NSRange, replacementString
string: String) -> Bool
```

The first method should clean the selected text field and all text fields after it.

The second method should make input validation. We allow only digits and only one per field.

To move focus from one field to another, we'll use the editingChanged action. Let's use a method called textChanged:

```
@IBAction func textChanged(_ textField: UITextField)
```

To make it easier, we can pack text fields into an array.

Recipe 6-15. Pin Pad

```
class PinPadViewController: UIViewController {
    @IBOutlet weak var digit1TextField: UITextField!
    @IBOutlet weak var digit2TextField: UITextField!
    @IBOutlet weak var digit3TextField: UITextField!
    @IBOutlet weak var digit4TextField: UITextField!
```

```swift
    private var pinDigitTextFields: [UITextField] = []

    override func viewDidLoad() {
        super.viewDidLoad()

        pinDigitTextFields = [
            digit1TextField,
            digit2TextField,
            digit3TextField,
            digit4TextField
        ]
    }

    override func viewDidAppear(_ animated: Bool) {
        super.viewDidAppear(animated)

        clear()
    }

    @IBAction func textChanged(_ textField: UITextField) {
        if textField.tag == 3 {
            view.endEditing(true)
            validateAndGo()
        } else {
            pinDigitTextFields[textField.tag +
            1].becomeFirstResponder()
        }
    }

    private func clear() {
        pinDigitTextFields.forEach {
            $0.text = ""
        }
        digit1TextField.becomeFirstResponder()
    }
```

```swift
    private func getPin() -> String {
        let digit1 = digit1TextField.text ?? ""
        let digit2 = digit2TextField.text ?? ""
        let digit3 = digit3TextField.text ?? ""
        let digit4 = digit4TextField.text ?? ""

        return "\(digit1)\(digit2)\(digit3)\(digit4)"
    }

    private func validateAndGo() {
        let pin = getPin()

        if pin.count != 4 {
            clear()
            return
        }

        // Here you can send PIN to API to verify it (or do it
            locally)
    }
}

extension PinPadViewController: UITextFieldDelegate {
    func textFieldShouldBeginEditing(_ textField: UITextField)
    -> Bool {
        for i in textField.tag..<3 {
            pinDigitTextFields[i].text = ""
        }
        return true
    }

    public func textField(_ textField: UITextField,
    shouldChangeCharactersIn range: NSRange, replacementString
    string: String) -> Bool {
        if let text = textField.text,
```

```
        let textRange = Range(range, in: text) {
         let updatedText = text.replacingCharacters(in:
         textRange,
                                              with: string)

         if updatedText.count > 1 {
            return false
         }
         if !updatedText.containsOnlyDigits {
            return false
         }

         return true
      }

      return false
   }
}
```

You should make validation in method validateAndGo.

There are always many ways to implement one feature or another. This is a very simple way; it can be more complicated if you need visual effects or decorations.

Summary

In this chapter we described how to validate text while editing, how to block some characters from user input, how to add prefix or suffix to text field. As most of mobile devices don't have keyboard, we should never forget about on-screen keyboard covering part of our user interface. To handle it, we need to subscribe to notifications and update layout. We also need to remember to hide keyboard when screen is changed. The last recipe shows one interesting use case of text fields – pin pad. Component for entering pin code or verification code from SMS. In the next chapter we'll finish discussing UIKit and talk about animations and visual effects.

CHAPTER 7

UI Animation and Effects

Animations and effects are important elements/aspects of modern mobile apps. Each app has dozens of similar apps available in the stores/gallery; you need to make yours stand out so customers will download yours. Beautiful animated UI helps it stand out.

We will review the most popular animation types:

- Moving `UIView` from one point to another, (e.g., when the keyboard appears/disappears)

- Animating properties like color or transparency

- Parallax effect with `UIScrollView`, `UITableView`, or `UICollectionView`

- "Hero" animation – moving the item from one view to another

- Overriding default transition between `UIViewControllers`

Animating Views

`UIView` and its subclasses have several properties that can be animated. We will split them into two groups:

© Alexander Nekrasov 2022
A. Nekrasov, *Swift Recipes for iOS Developers*,
https://doi.org/10.1007/978-1-4842-8098-0_7

- Animating own properties of views, like color, transparency, or scale

- Animating layout by changing constraints

Animating UIView's Own Properties

The most popular animation of UIView is "fade". "Fade in" makes UIView appear; "fade out" makes it disappear. What is appearing and disappearing? It's changing alpha property from 0.0 to 1.0 and back. Why do we change alpha instead of isHidden? It's a *Boolean* value. *Boolean* values cannot gradually change. They're always either true or false. Will this animation work anyway? Well, try it as an exercise. We'll stick to alpha here, as it's a gradually changeable property.

Animation can be done using UIView type animation (withDuration:animations:). It's a type method, so you call it directly on type UIView, not on instance.

Let's see how it looks in code. Make UIView or any subclass an outlet fadeView. Be careful, don't name it just view because it's reserved for root view (Recipe 7-1).

Recipe 7-1. Fade-in Effect

```
class FadeInViewController: UIViewController {
    @IBOutlet weak var fadeView: UIView!

    func fadeIn() {
        fadeView.isHidden = false
        fadeView.alpha = 1.0

        UIView.animate(withDuration: 0.3) {
            self.fadeView.alpha = 0.0
        }
    }
}
```

Before performing an animation, we set initial parameters. It's not compulsory, especially if you want to animate it from its current state. Adjust it for your needs.

You can also see a magic number in this recipe – 0.3. Magic numbers are unnamed numeric constants. It's a bad practice because the developer working on this code after you (or even you in several months or years) may not understand why this constant is there and what it means.

We're talking about animation, and this code is part of the book, so it's acceptable to give an explanation here. 0.3 seconds is a common time interval for animations. It's slow enough to let the user see it, but fast enough not to delay them.

If you use this code, adjust this time interval for your needs and define a named constant for it.

In Recipe 7-2 we have another version of animate method:

```
func animate(with Duration:animations:completion:)
```

Recipe 7-2. Fade-Out Effect

```
class FadeOutViewController: UIViewController {
    @IBOutlet weak var fadeView: UIView!

    func fadeOut() {
        fadeView.alpha = 0.0
        fadeView.isHidden = false

        UIView.animate(withDuration: 0.3) {
            self.fadeView.alpha = 1.0
        } completion: { _ in
            self.fadeView.isHidden = true
        }
    }
}
```

`UIView` object can animate the following properties:

- Frame

- Bounds

- Center

- Transform

- Alpha

- BackgroundColor

Subclasses of `UIView` may have other properties to animate; you can refer to documentation to see a full list for each class.

Animating Layout by Changing Constraints

When iPhone just appeared, it had only one resolution. Later, when new models appeared, screen became taller. On iPad, the opposite, it became wider. Now we have many aspect ratios. The way to survive in all this variety is to use constraints. If you're reading this, you probably already know what are constraints. If not, you can always find documentation, books, articles, or tutorials explaining how they work.

If you have constraints, you shouldn't animate frame and other position-related properties. You should animate changes in constraints.

To animate a constraint, you should make an outlet first. Let's say, we have some `UIView`, and we need to move it up. It has a constraint defining distance with an object on top. By default, it's 50, but we want it to be 20. Why? Maybe the keyboard appeared, or something else happened that we need to shrink our spaces.

```
@IBOutlet weak var distanceConstraint: NSLayoutConstraint!
```

Note   Up to the present day, constraints are objects of class NSLayoutConstraint; it starts with NS, and it doesn't have an alternative.

Here's the trick. Layout changes aren't performed when you change the constraint properties. They're performed when view is getting laid out. We need to prepare new layout *before* calling animate(withDuration:anim ations:). And in this method, we only call layoutIfNeeded of a parent or root UIView. You can see how it's done in Recipe 7-3.

Recipe 7-3. Animating Constraints

```
class AnimatedConstraintsViewController: UIViewController {
    @IBOutlet weak var distanceConstraint: NSLayoutConstraint!

    func changeDistanceAnimated(_ newDistance: CGFloat) {
        distanceConstraint.constant = newDistance
        UIView.animate(withDuration: 0.3) {
            self.view.layoutIfNeeded()
        }
    }
}
```

Restrictions

Animations in iOS have their own restrictions. We already discussed that you can't animate values that can't be gradually changed.

Another restriction is simultaneous animations. You can animate several properties or different objects at the same time, but they must be wrapped into the same block.

If you have complex animations, you have two solutions:

- Split them into small blocks, each of them with a set of changes ending at the same moment. When one block ends, start the next block. It may need some calculating.

- Make a timer to animate manually. The `UIView.animate(withDuration:animations`☺ method is not the only way.

Animating Layout When Keyboard Appears

In the "Keyboard Handling" section in Chapter 6, we discussed changes in keyboard layout. We changed a constraint without animation:

```
if let keyboardSize = (notification.userInfo?[UIResponder.
keyboardFrameEndUserInfoKey] as? NSValue)?.cgRectValue.size {
bottomConstraint.constant = keyboardSize.height
    view.layoutIfNeeded()}
```

In Recipe 7-4 we improve the code to make it look smoother.

Recipe 7-4. Animating Layout Changes When Keyboard Appears

```
class AnimatedKeyboardListenerViewController:
UIViewController {
    @IBOutlet weak var bottomConstraint: NSLayoutConstraint!

    override func viewWillAppear(_ animated: Bool) {
        super.viewWillAppear(animated)

        NotificationCenter.default.addObserver(
            self,
            selector: #selector(keyboardWillShow(notification:)),
```

```
        name: UIResponder.keyboardWillShowNotification,
        object: nil
    )
    NotificationCenter.default.addObserver(
        self,
        selector: #selector(keyboardWillHide),
        name: UIResponder.keyboardWillHideNotification,
        object: nil
    )
}

override func viewDidDisappear(_ animated: Bool) {
    NotificationCenter.default.removeObserver(self, name:
    UIResponder.keyboardWillShowNotification, object: nil)
    NotificationCenter.default.removeObserver(self, name:
    UIResponder.keyboardWillHideNotification, object: nil)

    super.viewWillDisappear(animated)
}

@objc func keyboardWillShow(notification: NSNotification) {
    if let keyboardSize = (notification.
    userInfo?[UIResponder.keyboardFrameEndUserInfoKey] as?
    NSValue)?.cgRectValue.size {
        bottomConstraint.constant = keyboardSize.height
        UIView.animate(withDuration: 0.3) {
            self.view.layoutIfNeeded()
        }
    }
}
```

```
@objc func keyboardWillHide() {
    bottomConstraint.constant = 0
    UIView.animate(withDuration: 0.3) {
        self.view.layoutIfNeeded()
    }
}
```

Note   Recipe 7-4 is almost identical to Recipe 6-13. The only difference is animation. Compare them.

Parallax Effect

Parallax effect in general is creating several layers moving with different speeds. This effect is often used in 2D platformer games or runners. Clouds behind the player move much slower than the player themselves. At the same time, the front layer covering the character moves faster.

In mobile apps, the parallax effect is often used as a screen header when content is scrollable. It can be a food ordering app, showing the restaurant photo above the menu. When the user scrolls the menu, the header should become smaller, leaving the back button and restaurant name, possibly with the restaurant logo or a card icon.

The parallax scrolling effect is not only moving from point A to point B, but it should also be responsive. The header should dynamically change when the user scrolls up and down (Figure 7-1).

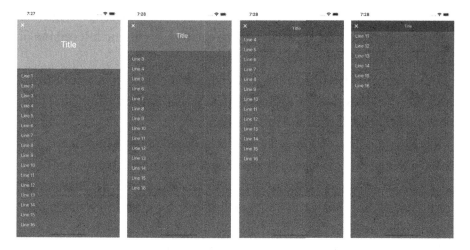

Figure 7-1. *Parallax effect*

Parallax Header with UIScrollView

A big part of this feature is the user interface, so let's prepare it first.

Preparing User Interface

In this example, we'll use a header containing the following objects:

- UIImageView on the background. *Content mode* should be set to *Aspect Fill*. This way, the background image will scale automatically, leaving only part of the picture visible, but it will always fill the whole screen.

- UIView shading. Background color will be black, but transparency (alpha) will change from 0.3 to 0.8.

- UIButton will be a static back button, always located in the top-left corner of the header.

- UILabel will display a title. Large and centered when the header is expanded and small when the header is shrunk.

295

When the user scrolls `UIScrollView`, the header will change height from 180 to 40. Scrolling back will reverse the process. In the full version of code, all numbers will be declared as constants.

The `UIScrollView` object should be located behind the header; otherwise, it will overlap the entire header. At the same time, we can't put it below. This needs a detailed explanation.

If our scrollable area is located below the header, its position and size will change every time the header height is changed. As the user's finger won't move, it will change its position in a scrollable area system of coordinates. It may look good, but usually it creates undesired shaking of scrolling offset.

Finally, we need to add some content to the scrollable area. Don't forget that it must have the margin from the top border, at least 180; otherwise, it will be hidden behind the header. If you want to scroll the bar, you should also add an inset in the Indicator Insets section in the storyboard editor. If not, hide it.

If you're done with storyboard editing, create the following outlets:

```
// Views
@IBOutlet weak var scrollView: UIScrollView!
@IBOutlet weak var headerView: UIView!
@IBOutlet weak var shadeView: UIView!
@IBOutlet weak var titleLabel: UILabel!

// Layout constraints
@IBOutlet weak var headerHeightConstraint: NSLayoutConstraint!
@IBOutlet weak var titleLeadingConstraint: NSLayoutConstraint!
```

Starting values of constraints, alpha, font, and other parameters should be the following:

- shadeView.alpha is 0.3.

- titleLabel.font is UIFont.systemFont(ofSize: 32).

- headerHeightConstraint.constaint is 180.

- titleLeadingConstraint.constaint is 16.

If the layout is too complicated, and you can't build it using this instruction, you can find an example in the GitHub repository.

Parallax Functionality

We need to set a delegate of UIScrollView. It will be our UIViewController. This method is called for every time the scroll position is changed:

```
func scrollViewDidScroll(_ scrollView: UIScrollView)
```

The current scroll position is

```
let scrollPosition = scrollView.contentOffset.y
```

To calculate all the values, we need to know current progress, which is a value from 0.0 to 1.0, where 0.0 is fully expanded and 1.0 is fully shrunk. How do we calculate shrink progress from scrollPosition?

We need to decide the speed. The header range is 180 - 40 = 140. We could change from 0.0 to 1.0 when the user scrolls it by 140 pixels, but we're building parallax effect, not another section in UIScrollView. Let's make it scroll half as slow. To make it happen, we need to divide scrollPosition by 280. Recipe 7-5 shows the full version of parallax effect code.

Recipe 7-5. Parallax Effect

```
class ParallaxViewController: UIViewController {
    // Views
    @IBOutlet weak var scrollView: UIScrollView!
    @IBOutlet weak var headerView: UIView!
    @IBOutlet weak var shadeView: UIView!
    @IBOutlet weak var titleLabel: UILabel!
```

```swift
// Layout constraints
@IBOutlet weak var headerHeightConstraint: NSLayoutConstraint!
@IBOutlet weak var titleLeadingConstraint: NSLayoutConstraint!

func setHeaderShrinkProgress(_ progress: CGFloat) {
    let progressClamped = max(min(progress, 1.0), 0.0)

    headerHeightConstraint.constant =
        ParallaxViewController.maxHeaderHeight * (1.0 -
        progressClamped) +
        ParallaxViewController.minHeaderHeight *
        progressClamped

    titleLeadingConstraint.constant =
        ParallaxViewController.maxLabelOffset *
        progressClamped +
        ParallaxViewController.minLabelOffset * (1.0 -
        progressClamped)

    titleLabel.font = UIFont.systemFont(
        ofSize: ParallaxViewController.minTitleFontSize *
        progressClamped +
        ParallaxViewController.maxTitleFontSize * (1.0 -
        progressClamped))

    shadeView.alpha =
        ParallaxViewController.minShadeAlpha * (1.0 -
        progressClamped) +
        ParallaxViewController.maxShadeAlpha *
        progressClamped

    headerView.layoutIfNeeded()
}
```

```
    static let minHeaderHeight = CGFloat(40)
    static let maxHeaderHeight = CGFloat(180)
    static let minTitleFontSize = CGFloat(14)
    static let maxTitleFontSize = CGFloat(32)
    static let minLabelOffset = CGFloat(16)
    static let maxLabelOffset = CGFloat(56)
    static let minShadeAlpha = CGFloat(0.3)
    static let maxShadeAlpha = CGFloat(0.8)
}

extension ParallaxViewController: UIScrollViewDelegate {
    func scrollViewDidScroll(_ scrollView: UIScrollView) {
        let scrollPosition = scrollView.contentOffset.y
        let progress = scrollPosition / 280.0
        setHeaderShrinkProgress(progress)
    }
}
```

Congratulations! This is our working parallax header. Method setHeaderShrinkProgress is just doing math using the same formula:

```
finalValue = expandedValue * (1.0 - progress) + shrinkedValue *
progress
```

To make sure all our values stay in range, we clamp progress, limiting its values from 0.0 to 1.0 in the first line.

Parallax Header with UITableView and UICollectionView

Having code for parallax effect with UIScrollView, we can easily make parallax effect with UITableView or UICollectionView. The thing is that both of these views are subclasses of UIScrollView, so when you set a delegate, it automatically sets UIScrollViewDelegate.

Still, we need to make some changes both in the code and in the storyboard.

First, change UIScrollView to UITableView. Add indicator inset like you did before and create a cell prototype to make some demo content. In the following recipe, it's just one UILabel with tag property equal to 1.

Then we need to add content inset:

```
tableView.contentInset = UIEdgeInsets(top:
ParallaxTableViewController.maxHeaderHeight, left: 0, bottom:
0, right: 0)
```

Progress calculation is also changed, as now it counts from -180, not from 0.

```
func scrollViewDidScroll(_ scrollView: UIScrollView)
{ let scrollPosition = scrollView.contentOffset.y
    let progress = (scrollPosition +
    ParallaxTableViewController.maxHeaderHeight) / 280.0
    setHeaderShrinkProgress(progress)}
```

And finally, we need to implement UITableViewDataSource. Don't forget to set both delegate and dataSource. Recipe 7-6 has the final code:

Recipe 7-6. Parallax Effect with UITableView

```
class ParallaxTableViewController: UIViewController {
    // Views
    @IBOutlet weak var tableView: UIScrollView!
    @IBOutlet weak var headerView: UIView!
    @IBOutlet weak var shadeView: UIView!
    @IBOutlet weak var titleLabel: UILabel!

    // Layout constraints
    @IBOutlet weak var headerHeightConstraint: NSLayoutConstraint!
    @IBOutlet weak var titleLeadingConstraint: NSLayoutConstraint!
```

```swift
override func viewDidLoad() {
    super.viewDidLoad()

    tableView.contentInset = UIEdgeInsets(
        top: ParallaxTableViewController.maxHeaderHeight,
        left: 0,
        bottom: 0, right: 0)
}

func setHeaderShrinkProgress(_ progress: CGFloat) {
    let progressClamped = max(min(progress, 1.0), 0.0)

    headerHeightConstraint.constant =
        ParallaxTableViewController.maxHeaderHeight *
        (1.0 - progressClamped) +
        ParallaxTableViewController.minHeaderHeight *
        progressClamped

    titleLeadingConstraint.constant =
        ParallaxTableViewController.maxLabelOffset *
        progressClamped +
        ParallaxTableViewController.minLabelOffset * (1.0 -
        progressClamped)

    titleLabel.font = UIFont.systemFont(
        ofSize: ParallaxTableViewController.
        minTitleFontSize * progressClamped +
        ParallaxTableViewController.maxTitleFontSize *
        (1.0 - progressClamped))

    shadeView.alpha =
        ParallaxTableViewController.minShadeAlpha * (1.0 -
        progressClamped) +
        ParallaxTableViewController.maxShadeAlpha *
        progressClamped
```

```
        headerView.layoutIfNeeded()
    }

    static let minHeaderHeight = CGFloat(40)
    static let maxHeaderHeight = CGFloat(180)
    static let minTitleFontSize = CGFloat(14)
    static let maxTitleFontSize = CGFloat(32)
    static let minLabelOffset = CGFloat(16)
    static let maxLabelOffset = CGFloat(56)
    static let minShadeAlpha = CGFloat(0.3)
    static let maxShadeAlpha = CGFloat(0.8)
}

extension ParallaxTableViewController: UIScrollViewDelegate {
    func scrollViewDidScroll(_ scrollView: UIScrollView) {
        let scrollPosition = scrollView.contentOffset.y
        let progress = (scrollPosition +
        ParallaxTableViewController.maxHeaderHeight) / 280.0
        setHeaderShrinkProgress(progress)
    }
}

extension ParallaxTableViewController: UITableViewDataSource {
    func tableView(_ tableView: UITableView,
    numberOfRowsInSection section: Int) -> Int {
        50
    }

    func tableView(_ tableView: UITableView, cellForRowAt
    indexPath: IndexPath) -> UITableViewCell {
        let cell = tableView.dequeueReusableCell(withIdentifi
        er: "DemoCell", for: indexPath)
        if let label = cell.viewWithTag(1) as? UILabel {
```

```
            label.text = "Line \(indexPath.row + 1)"
        }
        return cell
    }
}
```

Similarly, you can do it for `UICollectionView`.

Feel free to customize header effects. Add more elements; make movements nonlinear or whatever comes to mind.

Hero Animation

"Hero" animation is a view, "flying" from screen to screen, visually resembling a superhero (Figure 7-2). When you tap a photo, or a dish in a menu, it increases its size and changes its position, while other views change in background.

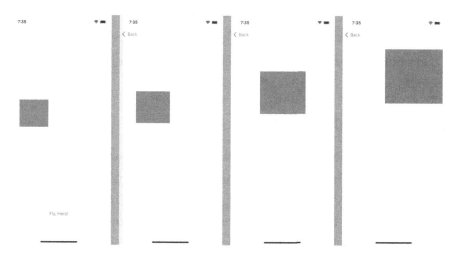

Figure 7-2. *Hero animation*

Hero Animation Within the Same UIViewController

Now, if we know how to make regular animations, we can create hero animation. To do it, we need to perform the following steps:

- Create and hide `UIView` in its destination point.

- Calculate the difference in position and size between source and destination points.

- Apply transformation to this `UIView` to make it look exactly like *source* `UIView`.

- Hide source `UIView` and show destination `UIView`.

- Animate destination `UIView` to return it to destination.

Assuming you don't rotate it, there are two transformations:

- *Translation* – Difference in position

- *Scale* – Difference in size

Let's build the entire algorithm, step by step; then wrap it up in a recipe.

Create and Show UIView

Hero animation is always the movement of an element, which looks the same but becomes larger. Original (source) `UIView` is smaller, so upscaling it will lead to quality loss. We need to create another `UIView`. Possibly, it's already created. In this case, we need to set it up. If you choose audio tracks with thumbnails, and the user selects one, you need to apply image and track name to the destination `UIView`.

At some point, we should have two `UIViews` (or subclasses), which look identical, but in different locations and with different sizes.

```
var destinationView: UIView
var sourceView: UIView
```

If you create it, make it hidden. If you have it in storyboard, it must be marked as hidden there.

Calculate Transformation

First, let's calculate the location in root view. If your sourceView and destinationView are both children of root UIView, you can skip this step.

```
let sourceCenter = view.convert(sourceView.center, to: nil)
let destinationCenter = view.convert(destinationView.center,
to: nil)
```

Then we need to calculate the distance between scales, horizontal and vertical.

```
let scaleX = sourceView.frame.width / destinationView.
frame.width
let scaleY = sourceView.frame.height / destinationView.
frame.height
```

Apply Transformation

On this step, we only apply a calculated transformation.

```
destinationView.transform = CGAffineTransform(scaleX: scaleX,
y: scaleY)
destinationView.center = sourceCenter
```

Hide Source UIView and Show Destination UIView

This is pretty straightforward. Until this step, destination UIView must be hidden.

```
destinationView.isHidden = false
sourceView.isHidden = true
```

Animate

Finally, we apply an animation the same way we reviewed earlier in the chapter.

```
UIView.animate(withDuration: 1.0)
    {destinationView.transform = CGAffineTransform.identity
    destinationView.center = destinationCenter}
```

That's it! Your hero can be a simple UIImage or a complex layout inside UIView.

Final Code

In Recipe 7-7, we simply have a UIView with background color. If you need a more complex structure, you'll have to duplicate it manually. There's no guaranteed way of copying a view structure in UIKit.

Recipe 7-7. Hero Animation

```
class HeroViewController: UIViewController {
    @IBOutlet weak var sourceView: UIView!
    @IBOutlet weak var targetView: UIView!

    @IBAction func animateHero() {
        let destinationView = UIView(frame: targetView.frame)
        destinationView.backgroundColor = sourceView.
        backgroundColor
        view.addSubview(destinationView)

        let sourceCenter = view.convert(sourceView.center,
        to: nil)
```

```
let destinationCenter = view.convert(destinationView.
center, to: nil)

let scaleX = sourceView.frame.width / destinationView.
frame.width
let scaleY = sourceView.frame.height / destinationView.
frame.height

destinationView.transform = CGAffineTransform(scaleX:
scaleX, y: scaleY)
destinationView.center = sourceCenter

UIView.animate(withDuration: 1.0) {
    destinationView.transform = CGAffineTransform.
    identity
    destinationView.center = destinationCenter
    }
  }
}
```

Also, we use another UIView – targetView. It's an invisible instance of
UIView, allowing us to set the geometry of destination in a storyboard.

Hero Flying to a New UIViewController

The difference between animation within the same UIViewController and
two different UIViewControllers is that we can't use destination UIView
from a storyboard.

The algorithm will be a little different:

- Run a segue or push destination UIViewController.
  Hide destination UIView on start.

- Create a transition UIView matching
  destination UIView.

- Calculate source and destination positions and scales.

- Add transition UIView to UIWindow and apply the source transformation.

- Hide source UIView.

- Apply animation of transition UIView's transformation. Transition between screens; the animation of UIView should be synchronous.

- When the animation ends, hide the transition UIView and show the destination UIView.

- Show the source UIView to make it visible when the user goes back.

Looks rather complicated, but it looks clearer in code. (Please find the currentWindow extension function in Recipe 4-3 or use the full version of Recipe 7-8 on GitHub.

Recipe 7-8. Hero Animation Between Screens

```
// In projects without scenes get window using this
code instead: (UIApplication.shared.delegate as?
AppDelegate)?.window

class Hero1ViewController: ViewController {
    @IBOutlet weak var sourceView: UIView!

    @IBAction func animateHero() {
        performSegue(withIdentifier: "Hero", sender: nil)
    }

    override func prepare(for segue: UIStoryboardSegue,
    sender: Any?) {
```

```swift
if let destinationVC = segue.destination as?
Hero2ViewController {
    guard let window = UIApplication.shared.
    currentWindow else {
        return
    }

    destinationVC.loadViewIfNeeded()
    destinationVC.view.layoutSubviews()

    let heroView = UIView(frame: destinationVC.
    destinationView.frame)
    heroView.backgroundColor = self.sourceView.
    backgroundColor
    destinationVC.destinationView.backgroundColor =
    self.sourceView.backgroundColor

    window.addSubview(heroView)
    self.sourceView.isHidden = true

    let sourceCenter = window.convert(self.sourceView.
    center, to: nil)
    var destinationCenter = window.
    convert(destinationVC.destinationView.center,
    to: nil)
    destinationCenter.y += self.view.safeAreaInsets.top

    let scaleX = self.sourceView.frame.width /
    heroView.frame.width
    let scaleY = self.sourceView.frame.height /
    heroView.frame.height

    heroView.transform = CGAffineTransform(scaleX:
    scaleX, y: scaleY)
```

```
            heroView.center = sourceCenter
            destinationVC.destinationView.isHidden = true

            UIView.animate(withDuration: 1.0) {
                heroView.transform = CGAffineTransform.identity
                heroView.center = destinationCenter
            } completion: { _ in
                destinationVC.destinationView.isHidden = false
                self.sourceView.isHidden = false
                heroView.removeFromSuperview()
            }
        }
    }
}

class Hero2ViewController: ViewController {
    @IBOutlet weak var destinationView: UIView!
}
```

Getting and Using UIWindow

In this recipe, we assume that the project uses Scenes. `currentWindow` computed property is defined in Recipe 4-3. If you don't use Scenes in your project, use Recipe 4-4 instead.

It may sound strange, but `UIWindow` is a subclass of `UIView`. That means we can use any `UIView` method on `UIWindow`. This includes `addSubview` and converse.

Details

Several more explanations to make it clear.

When destination `UIViewController` is created, view is not loaded. We need to do it manually:

```
destinationVC.loadViewIfNeeded()
```

We also need to layout views manually. Otherwise, they'll be in the same positions as in your storyboard editor. And it's not always the same after calculation. They match only when the device is the same as in your storyboard settings.

```
destinationVC.view.layoutSubviews
```

Another detail is that at the moment of calculation, the screen doesn't have any bars on top of the screen because the screen is not visible yet. So, the "y" coordinate of your destination UIView will be calculated incorrectly. Assuming that the top insets are the same on both screens, we make the following correction:

```
destinationCenter.y += self.view.safeAreaInsets.top
```

The rest of the code is basically the same as in the previous section with minor adjustments.

Transition Between Screens

By default, there are two types of animation:

- Appearing from right to left inside UINavigationController

- Appearing from bottom to top when you present a modal UIViewController

You can change animation in the "storyboard editor" or in code, but there's very limited choice. Luckily, iOS allows us to create a custom transition animation.

Standard Transitions

Depending on navigation type, there are two cases:

- If it happens inside UINavigationController, there is only one animation. The second screen covers the first one from the right side (or left side for right-to-left languages).

- When you present new `UIViewController` modally, there are several default options. We can choose the animation type in storyboard or in code before presenting.

If you use storyboards and segues, you need to choose the type of segue (*Show* for pushing and *Present Modally* for... presenting modally). Others are also used, but less often, and they have less customization options, so we'll set them aside for now.

The most interesting, from a transition point of view, is modal presentation. If you choose this type, you'll have two additional options:

- Presentation defines how the result looks. By default, it covers about 90% of the screen, leaving a piece of the previous screen on top.

- Transition defines the effect.

These options are accessible from code as shown in Recipe 7-9. You can instantiate the view controller from code or override parameters from segue.

Recipe 7-9. Changing Presentation and Transition

```
extension UIViewController {
    func openViewControllerDefinedWithStyle(destinationViewCont
    roller: UIViewController) {
        destinationViewController.modalPresentationStyle =
        .fullScreen
```

```
    destinationViewController.modalTransitionStyle =
    .crossDissolve
  }
}
```

Creating a Custom Transition

If you're not happy with standard animation, you can create your own custom transition.

When we're talking about custom transitions, we need to review several protocols:

- UIViewControllerTransitioningDelegate is a protocol you need to implement to make custom transitions. Implementation of this protocol defines animation and interaction controllers for presenting and dismissing.

- Implementation of the UIViewControllerAnimatedTransitioning protocol defines the duration of transitions and the transitions themselves and handles some callbacks.

- UIViewControllerContextTransitioning is a context. Implementation provides information about transitioning views and controllers.

When you implement the first two protocols, you need to set destinationViewController.transitioningDelegate. Let's see how it works, step by step.

1. When you trigger transition (using segue or manually), iOS checks if transitioningDelegate is set. If no, it uses one standard transition, the one you set or the default one.

313

2. If `transitioningDelegate` is set, it calls `anima
   tionController(forPresented:presenting:
   source)` of your `transitioningDelegate`. This
   function is optional; it's valid to return `nil`. If
   it does, the transition will be standard, like if
   `transitioningDelegate` wasn't set.

3. At this point, iOS concludes that custom animation
   must be used and creates a context.

4. `transitionDuration(using:)` is called to define
   transition time. Time should return in seconds.
   Usually, it's around 0.3 seconds. Transitions longer
   than one second will probably be uncomfortable
   for users.

5. Next, `animateTransition(using:)` is called. With
   this method, you can apply animations. Having
   context (in using argument), you can apply any
   modifications to both screens. You can change
   colors, positions, transparency – whatever you like.

6. Finally, you need to call `completeTransition(_:)`.
   This will mark transitions as over and make the
   destination view controller live. If you don't call it, it
   will remain inactive.

Some things are easier shown than explained, so let's have a look at
Recipe 7-10 to see how it looks in action. We'll make one of the simplest
transitions: the first screen will fade out, the second, fade in. In the middle
of the transition, there will be black screen because both screens will be
invisible. Animation duration will be one second, enough to see the entire
process.

Recipe 7-10. Fade Through Black Transition

```
class FadeThroughBlackPresentAnimationController: NSObject,
UIViewControllerAnimatedTransitioning {
    func transitionDuration(using transitionContext:
    UIViewControllerContextTransitioning?) -> TimeInterval {
        return 1.0
    }

    func animateTransition(using transitionContext:
    UIViewControllerContextTransitioning) {
        guard let fromView = transitionContext.
        viewController(forKey: .from)?.view,
            let toView = transitionContext.
            viewController(forKey: .to)?.view
        else { return }

        toView.isHidden = true
        transitionContext.containerView.addSubview(toView)

        UIView.animate(withDuration: 0.5) {
            fromView.alpha = 0.0
        } completion: { _ in
            fromView.isHidden = true
            toView.alpha = 0.0
            toView.isHidden = false
            UIView.animate(withDuration: 0.5) {
                toView.alpha = 1.0
            } completion: { _ in
                fromView.isHidden = false
                transitionContext.completeTransition(!transitio
                nContext.transitionWasCancelled)
            }
        }
```

```
        }
    }
}

class FromViewController: UIViewController,
UIViewControllerTransitioningDelegate {
    func animationController(forPresented
    presented: UIViewController, presenting:
    UIViewController, source: UIViewController) ->
    UIViewControllerAnimatedTransitioning? {
        FadeThroughBlackPresentAnimationController()
    }

    func animationController(forDismissed dismissed:
UIViewController) -> UIViewControllerAnimatedTransitioning? {
        FadeThroughBlackPresentAnimationController()
    }

    override func prepare(for segue: UIStoryboardSegue,
    sender: Any?) {
        segue.destination.modalPresentationStyle = .fullScreen
        segue.destination.transitioningDelegate = self
    }
}

class ToViewController: UIViewController {
    @IBAction func goBack() {
        dismiss(animated: true, completion: nil)
    }
}
```

This code includes backward transition, identical to the forward one.

Transition Libraries

If you want to create something new, look around – maybe someone created it already. There are many libraries offering transitions. Let's have a look at some of them:

- The Hero (`https://github.com/HeroTransitions/Hero`) library offers an easy way to apply one of the predefined transitions with a good set of tools for customizations.

- The Jelly (`https://github.com/SebastianBoldt/Jelly`) library also allows interactive transitions.

- Shift (`https://github.com/wickwirew/Shift`) is an animation library for hero-like transitions. With relatively little effort, it makes beautiful animations.

All these libraries are free, open source, and available via the Swift Package Manager and CocoaPods. You can use them free of charge in your apps, but don't forget to donate if you like them.

Summary

Modern mobile apps should use animations to look more user-friendly. UIKit offers native solutions for simple UI animations. In this chapter we discussed fade animations and animated layout changes. We talked about popular in mobile apps parallax effect, hero animation as a part of transition between screens. Finally, we reviewed different ways of transition itself. This wraps up UIKit topic, but UIKit is not the only way to create UI in iOS apps. Since iOS 13 Apple introduces SwiftUI, which is already actively used in both iOS and macOS UI development. In the next chapter we'll have a fast look at SwiftUI.

CHAPTER 8

SwiftUI

SwiftUI is a modern way of building user interfaces. It appeared in iOS 13, macOS 10.15, tvOS 13, and watchOS 6. Nowadays, most apps don't need to support iOS 12, so it's safe to use SwiftUI in your project.

On the other hand, there's huge code base written in UIKit. Hundreds of popular libraries appeared before SwiftUI or support old versions of iOS. That's why in this chapter, we'll talk not only about SwiftUI but also about mixing two frameworks.

What is SwiftUI? Is it a wrapper around UIKit or an independent platform? It's both. Some SwiftUI controls are built on top of UIKit; others are completely new.

Basic Overview of SwiftUI

SwiftUI uses the conception of building blocks. Each block is a View. Blocks can represent the whole screen, or part of it. Blocks can contain other blocks, and this structure can be deep. A similar architecture is used in other platforms like Flutter or React Native.

Basic App

SwiftUI apps contain two initial controls, App and View, shown in Recipes 8-1 and 8-2, respectively.

© Alexander Nekrasov 2022
A. Nekrasov, *Swift Recipes for iOS Developers*,
https://doi.org/10.1007/978-1-4842-8098-0_8

Recipe 8-1. SwiftUI App

```
import SwiftUI

@main
struct MyApp: App {
    var body: some Scene {
        WindowGroup {
            ContentView()
        }
    }
}
```

Recipe 8-2. SwiftUI View

```
import SwiftUI

struct ContentView: View {
    var body: some View {
        Text("Hello, world!")
    }
}

struct ContentView_Previews: PreviewProvider {
    static var previews: some View {
        ContentView()
    }
}
```

These two structs are the only pieces of code you need to run an app. It will have only one text label in the middle, but it will run.

Building Blocks

When you create a new SwiftUI project, you see two controls:

- Text – The closest control from UIKit is UILabel. Of course, it has SwiftUI specifics.

- ContentView – This View is the layout of the screen. It has size of phone screen because it's referred in your App struct.

From a SwiftUI point of view, there's no difference between Text and ContentView. For example, this code is totally valid:

```
@main
struct MyApp: App {
    var body: some Scene {
        WindowGroup {
            Text("I'm the only element on the screen :)")
        }
    }
}
```

At the same time, ContentView can be used inside another View. The most common controls are as follows:

- Text – A block of text similar to UILabel

- Image – A control displaying an image, similar to UIImageView

- HStack and VStack – Controls displaying a row or column of elements, one after another, similar to UIStackView

- List – A scrollable list of items, similar to UITableView or UICollectionView

- ZStack – A frame, showing child controls on top of each other, like `UIView` in `UIKit`

- Spacer – Used in stacks to make a dynamic gap between controls

- Button – A tappable element, allowing the user to control the app. Like `UIButton`

The preceding list is not a full list, but these controls are the most common.

Modifying Controls

You can make small modifications to controls without overriding them or creating new ones. For example, you may want to change the font, color, padding, background, and other properties.

In SwiftUI, it's done by calling methods following controls constructors. For example:

```
Text("Hello, world!")
          .font(.system(size: 14))
          .foregroundColor(.blue)
```

A modifier can be applied not only to components, but to a group of controls. For example, if you apply a foreground color to `HStack`, all the inner controls will get this color automatically, unless it's overridden.

Compositions

When you create a new control, you usually build it from existing blocks. This is a composition. SwiftUI has three main controls for this purpose:

- HStack – It shows controls horizontally one after another.

- VStack – It shows controls vertically one after another.

- ZStack – It shows controls on top of each other.

Recipe 8-3 is an example of such composition. It's a custom control for a guest list shown in Figure 8-1. You have a list of contacts with photos and names. On the right side, there's a switch. When it's on, the contact is invited; otherwise, they are not in our guest list.

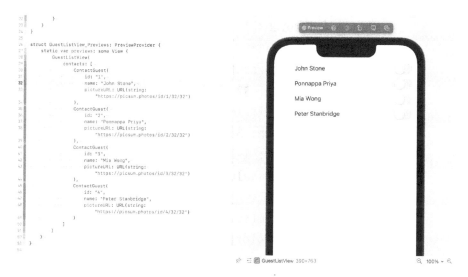

Figure 8-1. *Guest list written in SwiftUI. Code and preview*

Photos will be loaded from the Web using the URL provided in pictureURL. SwiftUI has a native AsyncImage control, but it's available only since iOS 15, so we'll use KFImage.

KFImage is a part of the Kingfisher library. You can add it using Swift Package Manager: https://github.com/onevcat/Kingfisher.

Recipe 8-3. Custom Component for Guest List

```
import SwiftUI
import Kingfisher
```

```swift
struct ContactGuestView: View {
    let name: String
    let pictureURL: URL?
    @State private var isInvited = false

    var body: some View {
        HStack(alignment: .center,
               spacing: 8.0) {
            KFImage(pictureURL)
                .resizable()
                .aspectRatio(contentMode: .fill)
                .frame(width: 32, height: 32)
                .clipShape(Circle())
            Toggle(name, isOn: $isInvited)
                .onChange(of: isInvited) { newValue in
                    print(newValue)
                }
                .font(.system(size: 16))
                .foregroundColor(.primary)
        }
        .padding(.leading, 16)
        .padding(.trailing, 16)
        .frame(height: 32, alignment: .center)
    }
}

struct ContactGuestView_Previews: PreviewProvider {
    static var previews: some View {
        ContactGuestView(
            name: "John Doe",
            pictureURL: URL(string: "https://picsum.
            photos/32/32")
```

```
    )
  }
}
```

Here's an interesting part in this line: `@State private var`
`isInvited = false`

It's a state of your component, or a part of it. When toggle (in UIKit, it's called Switch) state is changed, the variable is automatically changed too. You can access your state and take the necessary action.

How to handle state change? In an ideal case, we should have a view model that handles all the changes and stores the result in a repository. For this, we use method `.onChange`. Full signature looks this way:

```
@inlinable public func onChange<V>(of value: V, perform action: @
escaping (_ newValue: V) -> Void) -> some View where V : Equatable
```

In a provided closure, we change the value in the internal storage or send a request to the back end. In this example, we just print it.

Note   onChange should be called right after the Toggle declaration, before styling. Styling methods return simple View, not Toggle, which won't recognize the onChange method.

To wrap the SwiftUI basics up, Recipe 8-4 shows how to use it.

Recipe 8-4. Guest List

```
import SwiftUI

struct ContactGuest {
    var id: String
    var name: String
    var pictureURL: URL?
}
```

```
struct GuestListView: View {
    let contacts: [ContactGuest]

    var body: some View {
        ScrollView(.vertical, showsIndicators: false) {
            LazyVStack {
                ForEach(contacts, id: \.id) { contact in
                    ContactGuestView(
                        name: contact.name,
                        pictureURL: contact.pictureURL
                    )
                }
            }
        }
    }
}

struct GuestListView_Previews: PreviewProvider {
    static var previews: some View {
        GuestListView(
            contacts: [
                ContactGuest(
                    id: "1",
                    name: "John Stone",
                    pictureURL: URL(string: "https://picsum.
                    photos/id/1/32/32")
                ),
                ContactGuest(
                    id: "2",
                    name: "Ponnappa Priya",
                    pictureURL: URL(string: "https://picsum.
                    photos/id/2/32/32")
```

```
            ),
            ContactGuest(
                id: "3",
                name: "Mia Wong",
                pictureURL: URL(string: "https://picsum.
                photos/id/3/32/32")
            ),
            ContactGuest(
                id: "4",
                name: "Peter Stanbridge",
                pictureURL: URL(string: "https://picsum.
                photos/id/4/32/32")
            )
        ]
    )
  }
}
```

LazyVStack is a variation of VStack that doesn't render invisible components. LazyVStack inside ScrollView is like UITableView. SwiftUI has its own List, but when you have a static set of items, it may be faster to use this composition.

Inserting UIKit Components

SwiftUI is a relatively new framework. Most of the available libraries, including the popular ones, still don't support it. Fortunately, there's an easy way to insert standard UIKit UIView (or any subclass) to a SwiftUI component tree.

Creating a SwiftUI Component from a UIKit Component

Let's say you have a complicated custom `UIView` subclass `MyCustomOldView` that you're not ready to port to SwiftUI. You need to make a wrapper around it, which conforms to the `UIViewRepresentable` protocol.

The second step is to add properties. You can add them by adding variables to your struct.

Steps 3 and 4 are implementing two functions declared in the `UIViewRepresentable` protocol:

```
func makeUIView(context: Self.Context) -> Self.UIViewType
```

This function creates an instance of your `MyCustomOldView` and returns it. If there are any constant settings of that component, you can set them up in this function as well. It may be helpful if you're not using your own custom class, but standard UIKit class or class from an external library, and you need some adjustments.

```
func updateUIView(Self.UIViewType, context: Self.Context)
```

This function needs to update the state of your UIKit component. You shouldn't (re)create your `UIView` in this function; only apply all the changeable properties. Don't return anything.

Example with Custom Label

In Recipe 8-5, we'll wrap a `UILabel` subclass into a SwiftUI structure. Many apps have a predefined list of components with integrated styles and formatting. When the app starts working with SwiftUI, there are two options:

- To add all these components in SwiftUI using `Text`
- To wrap existing components into SwiftUI ones

The second way has an advantage if part of your app migrated to SwiftUI but another part didn't.

Recipe 8-5. Wrapping UIKit Components into SwiftUI

```
import UIKit
import SwiftUI

class HeaderLabel: UILabel {
    required init?(coder: NSCoder) {
        super.init(coder: coder)

        commonInit()
    }

    override init(frame: CGRect) {
        super.init(frame: frame)

        commonInit()
    }

    private func commonInit() {
        textAlignment = .center
        font = .systemFont(ofSize: 20, weight: .bold)
        textColor = .darkText
        numberOfLines = 1
    }
}

struct HeaderText: UIViewRepresentable {
    var text: String

    func makeUIView(context: Context) -> HeaderLabel {
        HeaderLabel()
    }
```

```
    func updateUIView(_ uiView: HeaderLabel, context:
    Context) {
        uiView.text = text
    }
}
```

Insert it in any SwiftUI View:

```
struct ContentView: View {
    var body: some View {
        HeaderText(text: "Hello, world!")
    }
}
```

If your properties can be changed dynamically, you can add the @ Binding keyword.

Applying Styles with ViewModifier

We already applied several styles with modifiers. We used font, foregroundColor, frame, and others.

When you create your own component, you don't have to provide all the adjustable properties in a constructor. It may be reasonable if you have two to three of them. But when you create a more complicated View, there can be dozens of them, and it's very uncomfortable to use them all in a constructor.

For this purpose, you can add extensions changing your custom View and view modifiers changing the properties of View more globally.

Creating a ViewModifier

To create your own modifier, you need to add a struct conforming to the ViewModifier protocol.

In this struct, you need to implement one function:

```
func body(content: Content) -> some View
```

In this function, you need to set up your View and return the result.

```
struct ModifierName: ViewModifier {
    func body(content: Content) -> some View {
        content
            ... // Do modifications here
    }
}
```

Chaining Modifiers in SwiftUI

To make your modifier look like the standard SwiftUI modifiers, you need to create an extension. Depending on your modifier, you can make it globally available by extending View, or make it more targeted to your own view or some tree of components (subclasses of Text, for example).

```
extension View {
    func applyMyStyle() -> some View {
        modifier(ModifierName())
    }
}
```

HeaderText without UIKit

Recipe 8-6 shows how we can make a modifier for Text to make a header with style matching the one from Recipe 8-5.

Recipe 8-6. HeaderText Using ViewModifier

```
import SwiftUI

struct Header: ViewModifier {
    func body(content: Content) -> some View {
        content
            .font(.system(size: 20, weight: .bold))
            .foregroundColor(Color(UIColor.darkText))
            .fixedSize(horizontal: false, vertical: true)
            .lineLimit(1)
            .frame(alignment: .center)
    }
}

extension Text {
    func styleAsHeader() -> some View {
        modifier(Header())
    }
}
```

Use it this way:

```
struct ContentView: View {
    var body: some View {
        Text("Hello, world!")
            .styleAsHeader()
    }
}
```

If there are properties specific to your View that can't be applied to Context, apply them in an extension directly, before calling the modifier method. For example:

```
func changeMyView() -> some View {
    doSomethingSpecific().modifier(SomeModifier())
}
```

Using ViewModifiers, you can create your own style library without subclassing Views.

Note   If you apply a modifier on a container (e.g., HStack or VStack), it applies to all of its children. That's why it's usually better to use pure modifiers without calling methods of the View subclass and to extend View globally.

Creating Custom Views

One of the most useful features of SwiftUI is creating custom reusable components. Creating small adjustable building blocks gives endless possibilities in UI creation.

There are three main ways of creating custom views:

- Composition of existing SwiftUI components adjusted for your needs

- Wrapping UIKit components

- Using Canvas for drawing your own views using lines, circles, and other primitives

Custom views can have changeable data. There are two key property wrappers:

- @State

- @Binding

We already discussed composition and wrapping UIKit components earlier in this chapter. Let's review `Canvas` drawing and property wrappers in details.

Drawing on a Canvas

Canvas is a SwiftUI control allowing to get access directly to CoreGraphics' `CGContext`. `CGContext` has a number of methods for drawing, such as follows:

- `func addRect(CGRect)` – Draws a rectangle

- `func addEllipse(in: CGRect)` – Draws an ellipse

- `func addArc(center: CGPoint, radius: CGFloat, startAngle: CGFloat, endAngle: CGFloat, clockwise: Bool)` – Draws an arc (part of an ellipse)

- And others

If we draw a filled circle with dashed border and spin it around its center, it can look like a loading indicator (see Figure 8-2). Let's review an example in Recipe 8-7.

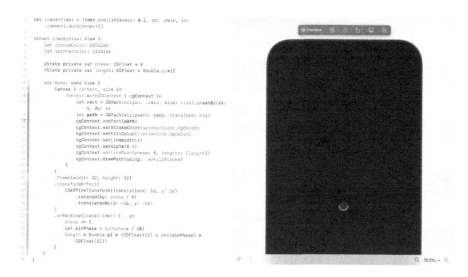

Figure 8-2. *Custom spinner written in SwiftUI*

Recipe 8-7. Using Canvas in SwiftUI

```
import SwiftUI

let loaderTimer = Timer.publish(every: 0.1, on: .main,
in: .common).autoconnect()

struct LoaderView: View {
    let circleColor: UIColor
    let spinnerColor: UIColor

    @State private var phase: CGFloat = 0
    @State private var length: CGFloat = Double.pi*12

    var body: some View {
        Canvas { context, size in
            context.withCGContext { cgContext in
                let rect = CGRect(origin: .zero, size: size).
                insetBy(dx: 4, dy: 4)
```

```
                let path = CGPath(ellipseIn: rect,
                transform: nil)
                cgContext.addPath(path)
                cgContext.setStrokeColor(spinnerColor.cgColor)
                cgContext.setFillColor(circleColor.cgColor)
                cgContext.setLineWidth(4)
                cgContext.setAlpha(0.5)
                cgContext.setLineDash(phase: 0, lengths:
                [length])
                cgContext.drawPath(using: .eoFillStroke)
            }
        }
        .frame(width: 32, height: 32)
        .transformEffect(
            CGAffineTransform(translationX: 16, y: 16)
                .rotated(by: phase / 8)
                .translatedBy(x: -16, y: -16)
        )
        .onReceive(loaderTimer) { _ in
            phase += 1
            let sinPhase = sin(phase / 20)
            length = Double.pi * (CGFloat(12) + abs(sinPhase) *
            CGFloat(11))
        }
    }
}

struct LoaderView_Previews: PreviewProvider {
    static var previews: some View {
        ZStack {
            Color.black
                .edgesIgnoringSafeArea(.all)
```

```
        LoaderView(
            circleColor: .blue,
            spinnerColor: .white
        )
    }
  }
}
```

You can see many magic numbers here. Try to play with them to see how the result changes.

Component State

We already used the @State keyword in several recipes. What is @State and how does it change our View?

@State is a property wrapper, which means it generates some code behind the scenes. It creates a storage and moves our variable out of struct as it's a value type. It's recommended to make @State variables private and initialize them right after the declaration, without a constructor.

@State variables are used to keep the View state. Depending on component logic, it can be a text string, a Boolean value, a number, or a structure. @State variables can be directly used in layout, and even more, the layout can change them in response to the user's actions.

@State variables shouldn't be shared between objects. They're not observable, and their changes can't be handled by willSet or didSet. To run some code when the @State variable is changed, you can use three ways:

- Use UI control callbacks, like onChange or onEditingChanged.

- Use bindings.

- Use observable objects (e.g., your view model can conform to ObservableObject).

To see the @State wrapper in action, please review Recipes 8-3 and 8-7.

Data Binding

Using @Binding instead of @State allows you to have a more powerful connection between variables and UI elements using it and share state between objects.

If you use a view model and declare some variable there, you can set up a connection with UI elements passing the binding itself, not the value.

The advantages of this approach are as follows:

- When you change Toggle or type text, it will change the value directly in your view model. It's much easier to use it later.

- If a variable changes several UI components, they'll be automatically updated when the variable is changed.

For example, if some text field should appear only when Toggle is on, @State won't solve the problem, but @Binding will (Recipe 8-8).

Recipe 8-8. Using @Binding

```
import SwiftUI

class LoginViewModel: ObservableObject {
    @Published var login: String = ""
    @Published var password: String = ""
    @Published var rememberMe: Bool = false
}

struct LoginView: View {
    @Binding var login: String
    @Binding var password: String
    @Binding var rememberMe: Bool
```

```swift
    var body: some View {
        VStack {
            TextField("Login", text: $login)
            TextField("Password", text: $password)
            Toggle(isOn: $rememberMe) {
                Text("Remember me")
            }
        }
    }
}

struct LoginScreenView: View {
    @ObservedObject var viewModel = LoginViewModel()

    private var loginAvailable: Bool {
        !viewModel.login.trimmingCharacters(in:
        .whitespacesAndNewlines).isEmpty &&
        !viewModel.password.trimmingCharacters(in:
        .whitespacesAndNewlines).isEmpty
    }

    var body: some View {
        VStack {
            LoginView(
                login: $viewModel.login,
                password: $viewModel.password,
                rememberMe: $viewModel.rememberMe
            )
            Button("Login") {
                print("Your login: \(viewModel.login)")
                print("Your password: \(viewModel.password)")
```

```
                if viewModel.rememberMe {
                    print("We will remember you")
                } else {
                    print("You will be automatically
                    logged out")
                }
            }.disabled(!loginAvailable)
        }
    }
}

struct LoginView_Previews: PreviewProvider {
    static var previews: some View {
        LoginScreenView()
    }
}
```

In this recipe, we use both bindings and observable objects. By using a publishable view model and bindings, we can control the *Login* button (it becomes inactive when one of the fields is empty) with minimum code. We can also access the entered values from the *Login* button callback without referencing the text fields themselves.

These features show the power of SwiftUI and its advantages compared to UIKit (Figure 8-3).

```
class LoginViewModel: ObservableObject {
    @Published var login: String = ""
    @Published var password: String = ""
    @Published var rememberMe: Bool = false
}

struct LoginView: View {
    @Binding var login: String
    @Binding var password: String
    @Binding var rememberMe: Bool

    var body: some View {
        VStack {
            TextField("Login", text: $login)
            TextField("Password", text: $password)
            Toggle(isOn: $rememberMe) {
                Text("Remember me")
            }
        }
    }
}

struct LoginScreenView: View {
    @ObservedObject var viewModel = LoginViewModel()

    private var loginAvailable: Bool {
        !viewModel.login.trimmingCharacters(in:
            .whitespacesAndNewlines).isEmpty &&
        !viewModel.password.trimmingCharacters(in:
            .whitespacesAndNewlines).isEmpty
    }

    var body: some View {
        VStack {
            LoginView(
                login: $viewModel.login,
                password: $viewModel.password,
                rememberMe: $viewModel.rememberMe
            )
            Button("Login") {
                print("Your login: \(viewModel.login)")
                print("Your password: \(viewModel.password)")
                if viewModel.rememberMe {
                    print("We will remember you")
                } else {
                    print("You will be automatically logged out")
```

Figure 8-3. *Data binding in SwiftUI*

Summary

SwiftUI is a future of iOS UI development. The purpose of this chapter
is not to give a comprehensive SwiftUI course, it's too big topic for one
chapter. But we talked about several interesting concepts showing power
of SwiftUI, such as building user interface from building blocks, using
UIKit components in SwiftUI, using ViewModifier, Canvas and Binding.

Index

A

B

C

Printed in the United States
by Baker & Taylor Publisher Services